A BRIEF HISTORY OF ART

Publisher and Creative Director: Nick Wells
Senior Editor: Sarah Goulding
Picture Research: Melinda Revesz
Designer: Chris Herbert
Production: Chris Herbert, Claire Walker

FLAME TREE PUBLISHING
Crabtree Hall, Crabtree Lane
Fulham, London, SW6 6TY
United Kingdom

www.flametreepublishing.com

First published 2006

10 12 14 13 11

9 10

Flame Tree is part of the Foundry Creative Media Company Limited

The CIP record for this book is available from the British Library.

ISBN 978 1 84451 445 8

Every effort has been made to contact copyright holders. We apologize in advance for any omissions
and would be pleased to insert the appropriate acknowledgements in subsequent editions of this publication.

While every endeavour has been made to ensure the accuracy of the reproduction of the images in this book,
we would be grateful to receive any comments or suggestions for inclusion in future reprints.

Printed in China

A BRIEF HISTORY OF ART

Authors: Camilla de la Bédoyère, Ihor Holubizky, Dr Julia Kelly, Michael Kerrigan,

Dr James Mackay, William Matar, Tom Middlemost, Michael Robinson & Iain Zaczek

Raphael (Raffaello Sanzio) *School of Athens*

**FLAME TREE
PUBLISHING**

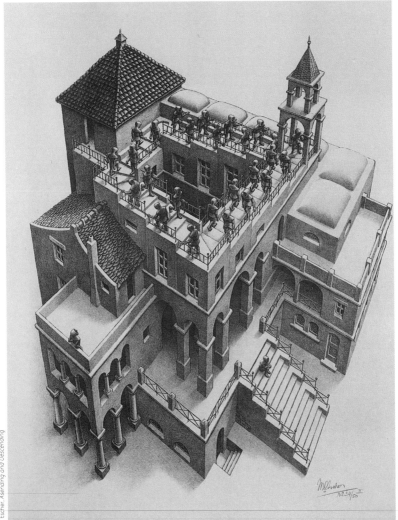

Contents

Hieronymus Bosch, *The Garden of Earthly Delights* (detail); Duccio di Buoninsegna, *Madonna and Child*; Jan van Eyck, *Portrait of Giovanni Arnolfini and Wife (Arnolfini Marr)*

Sandro Botticelli, *The Birth of Venus;* Titian (Tiziano Vecellio), *Venus and Adonis;* Giuseppe Arcimboldo, *Winter*

Albert Cuyp, *The Maas at Dordrecht with Fishing Boats*; Sir Anthony van Dyck (circle of), *Self Portrait with a Sunflower*; Jean-Honoré Fragonard, *Les Hazards Heureux de l'Escarpolette* ('The Swing')

Jean-Auguste-Dominique Ingres, *Jupiter and Thetis*; Eugène Delacroix, *Le Puits de la Casbah Tangier*; Caspar David Friedrich, *The Wanderer Above the Sea of Clouds*

Alfred Sisley, *Le Barrage de Saint Mammes*; James Whistler, *Nocturne: Blue and Silver – Chelsea*; Dante Gabriel Rossetti, *Reverie*

John William Waterhouse, *The Annunciation*; Paul Gauguin, *Nave Nave Mae*; Edvard Munch, *The Scream*

Wassily Kandinsky, *Composition No. 7*; Pablo Picasso, *Mandolin and Guitar – Juan les Pins*; Tamara de Lempicka, *La Musicienne*

How To Use This Book

The reader is encouraged to use this book in a variety of ways, each of which caters for a range of interests, knowledge and uses.

- The book is organized into seven ages: **Gothic & Medieval**, **Renaissance**, **Baroque & Rococo**, **Neoclassicism & Romanticism**, **Impressionism**, **Post Impressionism** and the **Modern Age**.
- The chronological format allows the reader to explore the progression and development of a style within each era.
- The format also enables the reader to discover unusual or unknown art amongst the more well-known artists of familiar periods.
- The text provides the reader with a snapshot of an artist's lifetime and allows further exploration of influences that can be discovered elsewhere in the book.
- The introduction gives an interesting perspective on our notion of what art is, and shows the reader how to gain more insight into a painting than merely appreciating it for its aesthetic appeal.
- The introduction also explains the different ages into which the book is split, and gives a little background to each one.

Turner, J. M. W.
The Burning of the Houses of Parliament
(detail), c. 1834–35

2. Name of artist, by surname then forename

3. Date of work (if known)

1. Title of work

9. Picture credit

4. Information about the work and the context within which it was created

8. Period or movement to which the work belongs

7. Similar works, either from the same or other artists, with similar styles, techniques or subject matter

6. Other artists who influenced the featured painter, or the medium in which the work was created (if known)

5. Biographical information about the featured artist: name, date and place of birth and date of death

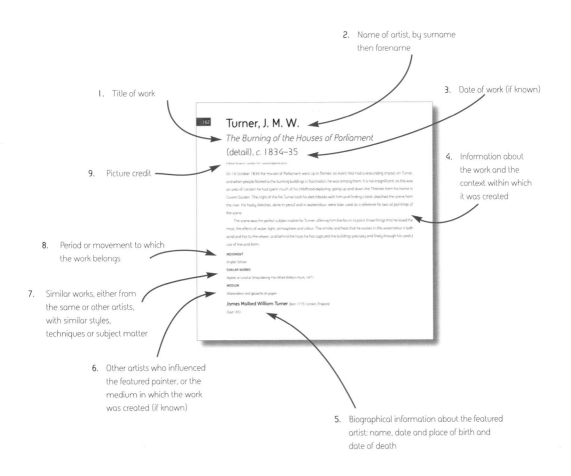

162 **Turner, J. M. W.**

The Burning of the Houses of Parliament (detail), c. 1834–35

© British Museum, London, UK / www.bridgeman.co.uk

On 16 October 1834 the Houses of Parliament went up in flames, an event that had a resounding impact on Turner, and when people flocked to the burning buildings in fascination, he was among them. It is not insignificant, as this was an area of London he had spent much of his childhood exploring, going up and down the Thames from his home in Covent Garden. The night of the fire Turner took his sketchbooks with him and finding a boat, sketched the scene from the river. His hasty sketches, done in pencil and in watercolour, were later used as a reference for two oil paintings of the scene.

The scene was the perfect subject matter for Turner, offering him the forum to paint those things that he loved the most, the effects of water, light, atmosphere and colour. The smoke and heat that he evokes in this watercolour is both acrid and hot to the viewer, and behind the haze he has captured the buildings precisely and finely through his careful use of line and form.

MOVEMENT
English School

SIMILAR WORKS
Naples or Land of Smouldering Fire Alfred William Hunt, 1871

MEDIUM
Watercolour and gouache on paper

James Mallord William Turner *Born 1775 London, England*

Died 1851

Paul Cézanne, *Still Life with Apples*, Courtesy of Private Collection/Bridgeman Art Gallery/Christie's Images

Introduction

For most people, the process of viewing something aesthetically pleasing can be a momentarily life-enhancing experience. The same people might also feel that there is a big difference between looking at a painting for its own sake, and accepting the concept of art as a medium conveying a set of intellectual theories and arguments. Many would ask why should we bother with art?

The enjoyment provided by the visual is an acceptable motivation in itself. However, it does not tell us very much about anything – after all, sweets can provide enjoyment too. Unlike sweets, though, art has the potential to enrich life in a manner that goes well beyond mere enjoyment, agreeable décor or a more superficial gratification through popular imagery. Moreover, because the art of our own time often simply reaffirms our own values and expectations, being familiar with the art of other times and places is a useful portal into the aesthetics, ideologies, morals, philosophies, politics and social customs of others. Art's most fundamental importance is perhaps not as décor but as an avenue of intellectual communication. This makes insight into art an invaluable part of an advanced comprehensive education.

A BRIEF HISTORY OF ART

Humankind has made images and marks since the dawn of time. Art predates history, as well as the current notion of what constitutes art. What we think of as art tends to be that art produced by urban civilizations, and more specifically, western urban civilizations. With the creation of the first art museum – the Louvre in Paris – a new world of art emerged that would establish a western hegemony on the idea of art and export it to the world. The world is a big place and art has increasingly taken on proportions unimaginable to the first art historians, leaving a daunting task to those who wish to revise that history, or add to it. Much of art has been mapped through individuals, forming schools and movements of type and style, and so the mapping approach of this book has been by chronology, stratified by regions of activity. The role of the art historian is to uncover the shape of time – cultural activity that is only known to us by the things we make, or the things that survive. That is what this book attempts to explore in the seven sections explained here.

THE GOTHIC & MEDIEVAL AGE

It was the art historian and pupil of Michelangelo, Giorgio Vasari, who coined the term 'Gothic' to describe the art and architecture of the Middle Ages, assuming that this style had originated with the Goths, the Teutonic barbarians who attacked the Roman Empire. Gothic thus came to represent the opposite of Classic (the art that derived from Greece and Rome). Strange as it may seem, Vasari's theories were not dismissed until the nineteenth century, and the label Gothic has remained to describe the fantastic spires and grotesque ornament of cathedrals, as well as the style in stained glass, tapestry and the applied arts. It found expression in the fine arts of the fourteenth and fifteenth centuries, mainly through the medium of the richly illuminated books of hours and other devotional works.

THE AGE OF RENAISSANCE

Renaissance, a French word meaning 'rebirth', alludes to the humanistic revival of the Classical influence in western Europe in the fourteenth to sixteenth centuries. Although the fall of Constantinople in 1453 and the consequent flight of the intellectuals to the west is often cited as the starting point of the Renaissance, the 'rebirth of learning' had begun several generations earlier as Arab arts and crafts filtered through Spain. It was marked by an unprecedented flowering of the arts and literature as well as the beginning of modern science. In the fields of the fine arts and architecture, the Renaissance had its greatest impact in Italy. Significantly it was in the great mercantile centre of Florence, rather than in the religious centre of Rome, that the movement developed initially, and it was in the liberal world of the merchant princes that the new art flourished most vigorously. Wealthy patrons like the Medici, Sforza and Strozzi families encouraged the art of da Vinci and Michelangelo, among others.

THE AGE OF BAROQUE & ROCOCO

A French word meaning 'irregular', Baroque was applied to a style in art and architecture very fashionable in the seventeenth century and distinguished by extravagant forms and ornamentation which became so elaborate as to verge on the grotesque. A new naturalism would later lead to greater realism and the vogue for landscapes in the eighteenth century. Rococo, fashionable in the same period, is an Italian term derived from the French rocaille ('rock work'), a word that describes the shell work decorating grottoes and rockery dells in

French gardens in the late seventeenth and early eighteenth centuries. The new style, with its asymmetrical curves, lightness and frivolity captivated the French and spread rapidly to Italy and other parts of western Europe. It reflected the spirit of the age, when beliefs in religious dogma and the divine rights of kings were constantly being challenged. In painting it was reflected in the love of nature and the rise of the landscape, but it also impacted on the great allegorical compositions – especially ceilings and murals.

THE AGE OF NEOCLASSICISM & ROMANTICISM

The discovery of the ruins of Pompeii in 1748 triggered off an interest in, and enthusiasm for, the antiquities of Greece and Rome. This was given direction by the German archaeologist and art historian Johann Joachim Winckelmann, who argued that beauty depended on calmness, simplicity and correct proportion, the complete antithesis of the Rococo, which was then at the height of fashion. Neoclassicism was an almost inevitable reaction to the frivolity of Rococo, and it was given a political dimension when it became the preferred style in France in the aftermath of the Revolution. A reaction against the sterile academic disciplines of Neoclassicism came towards the end of the eighteenth century with Romanticism, which began as a literary and philosophical movement and soon involved the fine arts. Individual aspirations, feelings, emotion and atmosphere were all emphasized, with the remote, the rugged and the exotic celebrated.

THE AGE OF IMPRESSIONISM

The term 'impressionism' was coined by the journalist Louis Leroy in 1874 and used in an article in the satirical magazine Charivari to attack the paintings of Claude Monet, which were exhibited that spring. The term derived, in fact, from one of Monet's canvasses simply entitled Impression: Sunrise, leading the critic to dismiss it as 'an impression of nature, nothing more'. The Impressionists took ordinary subjects and used colour to illustrate the play of light and shadow on surfaces to suggest rather than delineate faithfully what they saw. In its heyday, between the late 1860s and about 1879, Impressionism was a remarkable revolution against Classicism, seeking to achieve immediacy and spontaneity, playing on the emotions as much as the imagination to achieve results. It lingered on fitfully until the end of the century, spawning offshoots such as the Neo-Impressionism of Pissarro and the Pointillism of Seurat, but most of its practitioners moved on to Post-Impressionism.

THE AGE OF POST-IMPRESSIONISM

On the fringe of Impressionism was Paul Cézanne, who felt uneasy at the lack of discipline in this style and wished to return to a greater reliance on form and content without sacrificing the feeling for light and brilliant colours. Out of this evolved Post-Impressionism, a term that originally meant merely 'after Impressionism', but which became the springboard to all the varied 'isms' that that come under the heading of modern painting and which, accordingly, are described in the final section. Apart from Cézanne, the leading Post-Impressionists included Georges Seurat. Neither of them was particularly concerned with the emotional content of their paintings, but this was the principal feature of the lithographs and paintings of Henri de Toulouse-Lautrec and the works of Van Gogh and Gauguin.

THE MODERN AGE

Modernism is a general term used to cover a multiplicity of movements seen in retrospect as working towards comparable ends. As the twentieth century gathered pace, so society began to change ever more quickly. New art styles and movements appeared and disappeared equally rapidly. The advent of photography removed the need for artists to represent faithfully what they saw, giving rise to new forms of expression using myriad new and experimental techniques. Boldness and self-confidence were the keys to the artistic revolutions of the early twentieth century. The colourful abandon of the Fauvists, the staggering boldness of Cubism, the absurdity of Dada, the simplicity of De Stijl – developments like this were born of a deep conviction that it was up to art to define humanity's relation to its world. Understanding modern art, if indeed it can or is meant to be 'understood', is not just about reading its history or precedents but more about engaging with an ethos.

HOW TO READ THIS BOOK

You may find that you end up reading this book, or at least sections of it, more than once. Dipping into the entries selectively will allow you to be drawn into the subject of art through the artists, or pieces, that most appeal to you. Don't think of the book's selection of works as the final word on the subject – art history's canonical 'greatest hits', as it were. Think of them instead as exercises to prepare you for the great adventure of art – to explore a world that could never be encapsulated within the covers of one book.

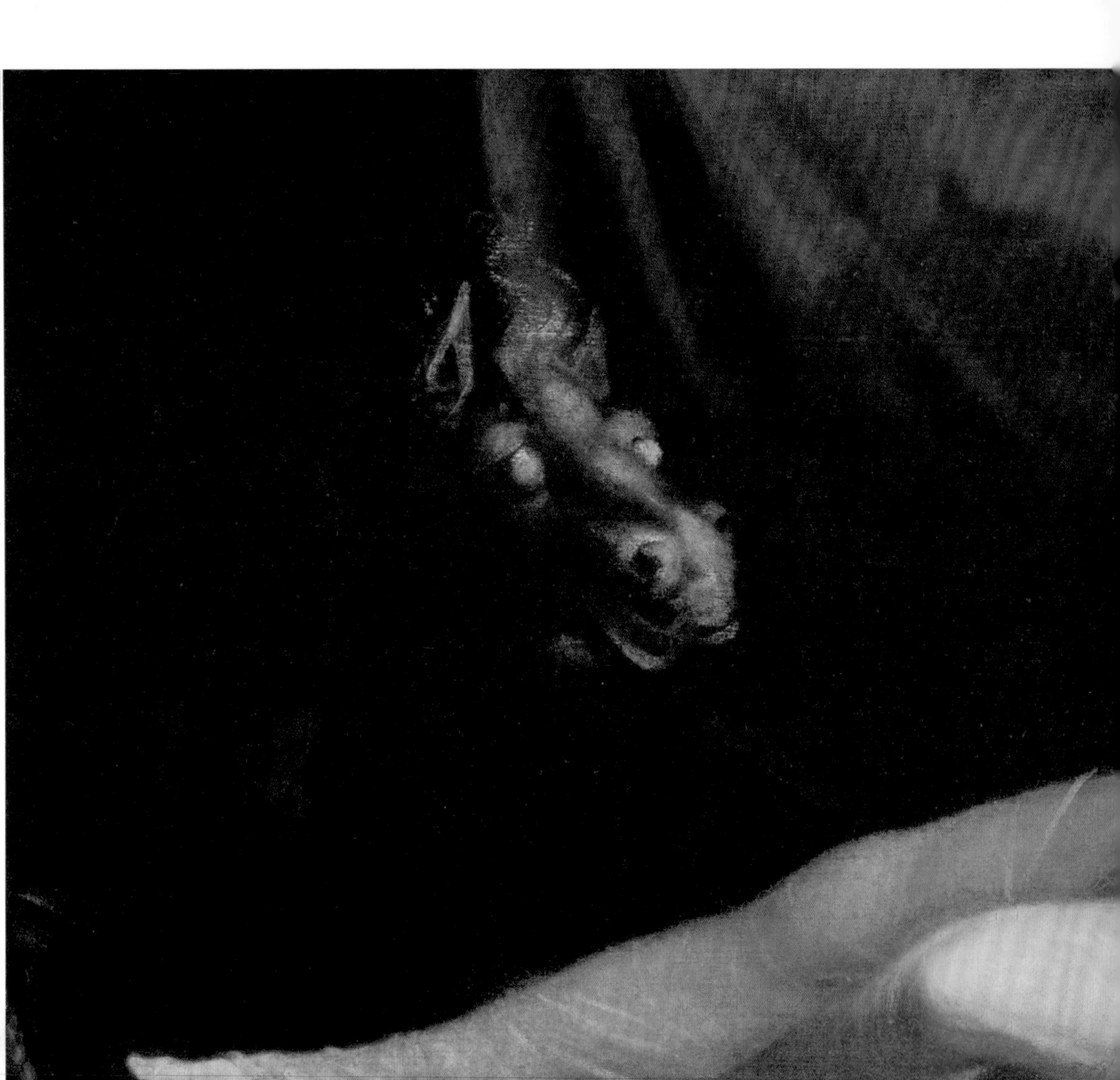

The Gothic & Medieval Age

1300–1500

Giotto (Giotto di Bondone)

Lamentation of Christ, c. 1305

Courtesy of Scrovegni (Arena) Chapel, Padua, Italy/Bridgeman Giraudon

One of the founding fathers of the Renaissance, Giotto was revered by early commentators as the greatest artist since antiquity, and it is clear that he was still influencing painters more than a century after his death. His greatest achievement was to rid Italian art of the repetitive stylizations deriving from Byzantine painting. In the process, he became one of the first Western artists to stamp his own personality on his work. In particular, Giotto displayed an unparalleled degree of naturalism, both in his ability to depict solid, three dimensional forms and in his grasp of human psychology. He was also a gifted storyteller, conveying his religious narratives with absolute clarity and simplicity.

The details of Giotto's own life are, however, a mystery. There is a tale that his master, Cimabue, first spotted his talent when he saw him as a shepherd-boy, sketching a lamb on a slab of rock. This is probably apocryphal, however, and the identification of Giotto's pictures presents even greater problems. The marvellous frescoes in the Arena Chapel, Padua, are usually cited as his masterpiece, but most other attributions are hotly disputed. Even his three signed altarpieces may only be workshop pieces.

MOVEMENT

Proto-Renaissance

OTHER WORKS

Arena Chapel Frescos; Madonna and Child; Ognissanti Madonna

INFLUENCES

Cimabue, Pietro Cavallini

Giotto *Born c. 1267 Italy*

Died 1337

di Buoninsegna, Duccio

Madonna and Child, (triptych detail) *c.* 1315

Courtesy of National Gallery, London, UK/Bridgeman Art Library

Western art begins with Duccio di Buoninsegna, who learned his craft from studying the illuminated manuscripts created by unknown Byzantine limners. His earliest recorded work, dating about 1278, was to decorate the cases in which the municipal records of Sienna were stored. In 1285 he was commissioned to paint a large Madonna for the church of Santa Maria Novella. This is now known as the Rucellai Madonna, for centuries attributed to Cimabue. Duccio painted the magnificent double altarpiece for the Cathedral of Siena, regarded as his masterpiece and one of the greatest paintings of all time. Many other works documented in the Sienese records have been lost, but sufficient remain to establish Duccio as the last and greatest of the artists working in the Byzantine tradition, as well as the founder of the Sienese School, and thus the progenitor of modern art. In his hands the degenerate painting of the Gothic style was transformed and the principles of expressive portraiture established.

MOVEMENT

Sienese School, Italy

OTHER WORKS

The Crucifixion; Majestas; Madonna with Three Franciscans

INFLUENCES

Byzantine illuminations

Duccio di Buoninsegna *Born c.* 1255 Siena, Italy

Died 1319

Master of the *Breviary of John the Fearless*

Breviary of John the Fearless, (detail of page)

c. 1413–19

With its dazzling colours and skilful use of gold, the manuscript of the *Breviary of John the Fearless* is a sumptuous example of the richly illuminated books of hours and other devotional works that proliferated during the height of the Gothic style. In this example, Christ appears to point the apostles to the Kingdom of God. The artist responsible for the illumination is known only by the moniker of 'The Master of the Breviary of John the Fearless', and there is no doubt that there were also contributions to the manuscript from 'associates'. However, it is clear that he was at least heavily influenced by the finest exponents of this art – the three brothers Pol, Hermann and Janneken Malouel from Limbourg in Flanders (now Belgium and the Netherlands), who flourished around the end of the fourteenth century.

MOVEMENT

International Gothic

OTHER RELEVANT WORKS

Très Riches Heures du Duc de Berri by the Limbourg Brothers

INFLUENCES

Gentile da Fabriano, Limbourg Brothers

van Eyck, Jan

Portrait of Giovanni Arnolfini and Wife (Arnolfini Marr), 1434

Jan van Eyck settled in Bruges in 1431, where he became the leading painter of his generation and founder of the Bruges School. He and his elder brother Hubert are credited with the invention of oil painting. Van Eyck's paintings have a startlingly fresh quality about them, not only in the dazzling use of light and colour but also in their expression and realism, which was something of a quantum leap in portraiture. Van Eyck was very much a pillar of the establishment, being successively court painter to John of Bavaria, Count of Holland, and Philip the Good of Burgundy. He was equally versatile in painting interiors and outdoor scenes, and exhibited a greater attention to detail than in the works of his predecessors. It is not surprising that he should not only sign and date his paintings but add his motto *Als ich kan* ('As I can').

MOVEMENT

Bruges School of Flemish Painting

OTHER WORKS

A Man in a Turban

INFLUENCES

Hubert van Eyck

Jan van Eyck *Born c.* 1389 Maastricht, Holland

Died 1441

Fouquet, Jean

The Nativity, c. 1445

The most representative French painter of the fifteenth century, Jean Fouquet originally came under the influence of van Eyck, but a period in Italy – where he was commissioned to paint the portrait of Pope Eugenius IV – brought him in contact with the new styles emerging in Tuscany. On his return to France he combined the Flemish and Tuscan elements to create a wholly distinctive French style. Highly influential on the succeeding generation of French artists, Fouquet's supreme importance was not fully realized until 1904, when his surviving works were brought together for an exhibition in Paris. His painting combines the skills and precision acquired during his early career as a limner and miniaturist with a new-found expressiveness that places him in the forefront of the painters who could get behind the eyes of their subjects and reveal the underlying character.

MOVEMENT

French Primitives

OTHER WORKS

Virgin and Child; Saint Margaret and Olibrius; Jouvenal des Ursins

INFLUENCES

Van Eyck, Piero della Francesca

Jean Fouquet *Born c. 1420 Tours, France*

Died c. 1481

Memling, Hans

Adoration of the Magi (central panel of triptych), *c.* 1470

Courtesy of Prado, Madrid, Spain/Bridgeman Art Library

Although born in Germany Memling spent most of his life in Bruges (now in Belgium), where he was probably a pupil of Rogier van der Weyden. This is borne out by the great triptych, whose central panel was painted by Rogier but the wings by 'Master Hans'. Bruges, which had been the commercial centre of the duchy of Burgundy, was then in decline and it has been said that Memling's genius alone brought lustre to the city. He was certainly residing in Bruges by 1463 and four years later enrolled in the painters' guild. In 1468 he painted the triptych showing the Virgin enthroned, flanked by the family of the donor, Sir John Donne, who was in Burgundy for the wedding of Charles the Bold that year. Although best known for his altarpieces and other religious paintings, Memling also produced a number of secular pieces, mostly portraits of his contemporaries. His paintings are characterized by an air of serenity and gentle piety enhanced by the use of vivid colours and sumptuous texture.

MOVEMENT

Flemish School

OTHER WORKS

The Mystic Marriage of St Catherine; The Virgin Enthroned

INFLUENCES

Rogier van der Weyden

Hans Memling *Born c. 1433, Germany*

Died 1494

Bosch, Hieronymus

The Garden of Earthly Delights
(central panel of triptych), *c.* 1500

Born Jerome van Aken but known by the Latin version of his first name and a surname from the shortened form of his birthplace 's Hertogenbosch in North Brabant, where he spent his entire life, Bosch painted great allegorical, mystical and fantastic works that combined the grotesque with the macabre. His oils are crammed with devils and demons, weird monsters, dwarves and hideous creatures, barely recognizable in human form. His quasi-religious and allegorical compositions must have struck terror in the hearts of those who first beheld them, but centuries later he would have a profound influence on the Surrealists. In more recent times there have been attempts to analyse his paintings in Jungian or Freudian terms, the theory being that he tried to put his more lurid nightmares onto his wood panels. This is his best known work, executed on four folding panels, in which he develops the story of the Creation and the expulsion of Adam and Eve. At the core of the work is a vast sexual orgy, symbolizing the sins of the flesh that caused man's downfall.

MOVEMENT

Surrealism

OTHER WORKS

The Temptation of St Anthony; Last Judgment

INFLUENCES

Gothic art

Hieronymus Bosch *Born c.* 1450, Hertogenbosch, Holland

Died 1516

The Age of Renaissance

1420–1600

Angelico, Fra (Guido di Pietro)
The Annunciation (detail), *c.* 1420

Courtesy of Prado, Madrid, Spain/Bridgeman Art Library/Christie's Images

Fra Angelico was one of a select band of Renaissance artists who combined the monastic life with a career as a professional painter. Little is known about his early years, apart from the fact that he was born at Vicchio, near Florence, and that his real name was Guido di Pietro. He became a Dominican friar *c.* 1418–21, entering the monastery of San Domenico in Fiesole. For the remainder of his life, he placed his art at the service of his faith, earning the nickname 'Angelic', by which he has become known to posterity.

Angelico's earliest surviving works are small-scale and betray an astonishing eye for detail, suggesting that he may have begun his career as a manuscript illuminator. They also display the influence of the International Gothic style, which was starting to fall out of fashion. The painter-monk learned quickly, however, absorbing Tommaso Masaccio's revolutionary ideas about the organization of space and perspective. He also tackled the most prestigious form of religious art: frescoe painting. In this field, Angelico's greatest achievement was a magnificent cycle of frescoes at the newly restored monastery of San Marco in Florence (*c.* 1438–45).

MOVEMENT

Renaissance

OTHER WORKS

Linaiuoli Triptych; Coronation of the Virgin

INFLUENCES

Masaccio, Monaco

Fra Angelico *Born c.* 1400

Died 1455

da Fabriano, Gentile

The Adoration of the Magi, detail of Virgin and Child with Three Kings, 1423

Courtesy of Galleria Degli Uffizi, Florence, Italy/Bridgeman Art Library

Born in the little north Italian town of Fabriano, Gentile worked as a painter mainly in Venice and later Brescia before settling in Rome in about 1419, although subsequently he also worked in Florence and Siena. There he executed a great number of religious paintings although, regrettably, comparatively few of these works appear to have survived. His most important work was probably carried out in Florence where he enjoyed the patronage of Palla Strozzi, the richest magnate of the city in his day. About 1423 Strozzi commissioned him to paint the magnificent altarpiece depicting the Adoration of the Magi for the sacristy-chapel in the church of the Holy Trinity, intended by the patron as a memorial to his father Onofrio Strozzi. This is Gentile's undoubted masterpiece. The very epitome of the Italian Renaissance, it is now preserved in the Uffizi Gallery. It is an extraordinary work, crammed with figures – among whom we may discern the Strozzi family and their friends.

MOVEMENT

Florentine School

OTHER WORKS

Madonna and Child; Madonna with Angels

INFLUENCES

Filippo Brunneleschi

Gentile da Fabriano *Born c. 1370 Fabriano, Italy*

Died c. 1427

Masaccio, Tommaso
Madonna Casini, 1426

Born Tommaso de Giovanni di Simone Guidi at Castel San Giovanni di Altura in the duchy of Milan, he was nicknamed Masaccio ('massive') to distinguish him from another Tommaso who worked in the same studio. Who taught him is not recorded, but Masaccio was one of the most brilliant innovators of his generation, ranking with Brunelleschi and Donatello in revolutionizing painting in Italy. Biblical figures and scenes became infinitely more realistic in his hands. The human body is more fully rounded than before and Masaccio's handling of perspective is a marked improvement over his predecessors. He wielded enormous influence over his contemporaries and successors, notably Michelangelo. His greatest work consisted of the series of frescoes for the Brancacci Chapel in the Church of Santa Maria del Carmine in Florence (1424–27).

MOVEMENTS

Italian Renaissance, Florentine School

OTHER WORKS

The Virgin and Child; The Trinity with the Virgin and St John

INFLUENCES

Donatello

Tommaso Masaccio *Born* 1401 Castel San Giovanni di Alturo, Italy

Died 1428

Gozzoli, Benozzo
Angels, c. 1459

Courtesy of K & B News Foto, Florence/Bridgeman Art Library/Christie's Images

Born Benozzo di Lese di Sandro, Gozzoli studied painting under Fra Angelico and assisted his master in the decoration of the Palazzo Medici-Riccardi in 1456–60. Gozzoli's major contribution was the *Journey of the Magi*, an ambitious work crammed with the portraits of the Florentine council and members of the Medici family. Later he moved with his master to Rome and later worked in Orvieto, also executing numerous frescoes and large murals for churches in Gimignano and Pisa. After leaving Angelico he went to Montefalco in Umbria, where he painted a number of smaller, individual works and altarpieces. As well as the obligatory religious subjects he painted a number of portraits, including Dante, Petrarch and Giotto. His paintings are characterized by their light, lively appearance, their vivacity enhanced by his use of bright, brilliant colours.

MOVEMENT

Florentine School

OTHER WORKS

St Thomas Receiving the Girdle of the Virgin

INFLUENCES

Fra Angelico

Benozzo Gozzoli *Born* 1420 Florence, Italy

Died 1497

da Messina, Antonello

Portrait of a Man, c. 1475

Courtesy of National Gallery, London/Bridgeman Art Library

Probably born at Messina, Sicily, whence he derived his surname, Antonello travelled in north-western Europe and spent some time in the Netherlands where he studied the techniques of the pupils of Jan Van Eyck, taking them back to Messina about 1465. Subsequently he worked in Milan and then, in 1472, settled in Venice, where he executed commissions for the Council of Ten. His paintings are remarkable for their blend of Italian simplicity and the Flemish delight in meticulous detail, although some of his earlier works do not always result in a perfect blend of techniques. The majority of his extant authenticated works are religious subjects, mainly painted in oils on wood panels, but he also produced a number of half-length portraits of Venetian dignitaries in the last years of his life. By introducing Flemish characteristics Antonello transformed Italian painting, notably in the use of oil paints, which revolutionized technique.

MOVEMENT

Italian Renaissance

OTHER WORKS

Ecce Homo; Madonna

INFLUENCES

Jan Van Eyck, the Flemish School

Antonello da Messina *Born c. 1430 Italy*

Died 1479

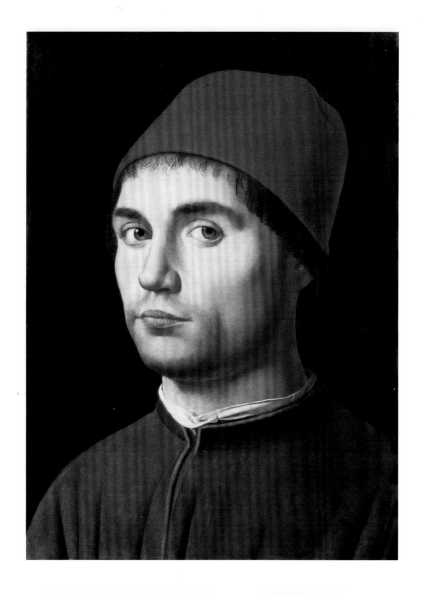

Botticelli, Sandro

The Birth of Venus, c. 1485

Courtesy of Galleria Degli Uffizi, Florence/Bridgeman Art Library/Christie's Images

Born Alessandro Di Mariano dei Filipepi, Botticelli acquired his nickname ('little barrel') from his brother Giovanni, who raised him and who was himself thus named. From 1458 to 1467 he worked in the studio of Fra Lippo Lippi before branching out on his own. By 1480 he was working on the frescoes for the Sistine Chapel and his lesser works consist mainly of religious paintings, although it is for his treatment of allegorical and mythological subjects that he is best remembered. Outstanding in this group are his paintings *Primavera* (1477) and *The Birth of Venus* (1485), both now in the Uffizi, Florence. He also excelled as a portraitist and provided the illustrations for Dante's *Divine Comedy*, which he executed in pen and ink and silver-point (1402–05).

MOVEMENT

Florentine School

OTHER WORKS

Venus and Mars

INFLUENCES

Fra Lippo Lippi, Verrocchio

Sandro Botticelli *Born* 1445 Florence, Italy

Died 1510

da Vinci, Leonardo

Mona Lisa, c. 1503–06

A Florentine painter, scientist and inventor and the supreme genius of the Renaissance, Leonardo da Vinci was the illegitimate son of a notary and probably trained under Verrocchio. In 1482 he moved to Milan, where he worked for the Sforzas. His chief work from this period was a majestic version of *The Last Supper*. The composition dazzled contemporaries, but da Vinci's experimental frescoe technique failed and the picture deteriorated rapidly. This was symptomatic of his attitude to painting: the intellectual challenge of creation fascinated him, but the execution was a chore and many of his artistic projects were left unfinished. Da Vinci returned to Florence in 1500, where he produced some of his most famous pictures, most notably the *Mona Lisa*. These were particularly remarkable for their *sfumato* – a blending of tones so exquisite that the forms seem to have no lines or borders. He spent a second period in Milan, before ending his days in France. Da Vinci's genius lay in the breadth of his interests and his infinite curiosity. In addition to his art, his notebooks display a fascination for aeronautics, engineering, mathematics and the natural world.

MOVEMENT

Renaissance

OTHER WORKS

Mona Lisa; Virgin of the Rocks; The Last Supper

INFLUENCES

Verrocchio

Leonardo da Vinci *Born* 1452 Italy

Died 1519

Michelangelo
Creation of Adam, Sistine Chapel detail, 1510

Courtesy of Vatican Museums and Galleries, Rome, Bridgeman Art Library/Christie's Images

Michelangelo was an Italian painter, sculptor and poet, one of the greatest artists of the Renaissance and a forerunner of Mannerism. He was raised in Florence, where he trained briefly under Ghirlandaio. Soon his obvious talent brought him to the notice of important patrons. By 1490, he was producing sculpture for Lorenzo di Medici and, a few years later, he began his long association with the papacy.

Michelangelo's fame proved a double-edged sword. He was often inveigled into accepting huge commissions, which either lasted years or went unfinished. The most notorious of these projects was the Tomb of Julius II, which occupied the artist for over 40 years. Michelangelo always considered himself primarily a sculptor and he was extremely reluctant to take on the decoration of the Sistine Chapel. Fortunately he was persuaded, and the resulting frescoes are among the greatest creations in Western art. The ceiling alone took four years (1508–12), while the Last Judgment (1536–41) was added later on the altar wall. In these, Michelangelo displayed the sculptural forms and the terribilità ('awesome power'), which made him the most revered artist of his time.

MOVEMENTS

Renaissance, Mannerism

OTHER WORKS

David; Pietà

INFLUENCES

Ghirlandaio, Giotto, Masaccio

Michelangelo *Born* 1475 Italy

Died 1564

Raphael (Raffaello Sanzio)

School of Athens, 1510–11

The archetypal artist of the High Renaissance, Raphael received his education in Perugino. In 1504 he moved to Florence, where he received many commissions for portraits and pictures of the Virgin and Child. Soon, his reputation reached the ears of Pope Julius II, who summoned him to Rome in 1508. Deeply influenced by Michelangelo he added a new sense of grandeur to his compositions and greater solidity to his figures. Michelangelo grew jealous of his young rival, accusing him of stealing his ideas, but Raphael's charming manner won him powerful friends and numerous commissions.

The most prestigious of these was the decoration of the Stanze, the papal apartments in the Vatican. This was a huge task, which occupied the artist for the remainder of his life. *School of Athens* is the most famous of these frescoes. Other commissions included a majestic series of cartoons for a set of tapestries destined for the Sistine Chapel and a cycle of frescoes for the banker, Agostino Chigi. In the midst of this frantic activity, however, Raphael caught a fever and died, at the tragically young age of 37.

MOVEMENT

Renaissance

OTHER WORKS

Galatea; The Sistine Madonna

INFLUENCES

Pietro Perugino, Leonardo da Vinci, Michelangelo

Raphael *Born* 1483 Urbino, Italy

Died 1520

Dürer, Albrecht

Melancholia, 1514

Albrecht Dürer was the son of a goldsmith who taught him the art of drawing in silver-point. In 1484 he was apprenticed to the leading Nuremberg painter and book illustrator of his time, Michael Wolgemut (1434–1519), from whom he learned the techniques of woodcut engraving. He then travelled extensively in Italy, where the works of Leonardo, Bellini and Mantegna had a profound influence on his later career, both as a practicing artist and as an art theorist who wrote extensively on the subject. Dürer was thus responsible for introducing many of the ideas of the Italian Renaissance to northern Europe. Although now remembered chiefly for his engravings (including the *Triumphal Car*, at nine square metres the world's largest woodcut), he was an accomplished painter whose mastery of detail and acute observation have seldom been surpassed.

MOVEMENT

German School

OTHER WORKS

Wing of a Hooded Crow

INFLUENCES

Leonardo da Vinci, Bellini, Mantegna

Albrecht Dürer *Born* 1471 Nuremberg, Germany

Died 1528

Correggio
Noli Me Tangere, c. 1534

Courtesy of Prado, Madrid, Spain/Bridgeman Art Library

Antonio Allegri, known to posterity by his nickname of Correggio, was born in the town of that name in the duchy of Modena. Originally he began training as a physician and surgeon, and studied anatomy under Giovanni Battista Lombardi – believed to be the doctor portrayed in the painting entitled *Correggio's Physician*. In 1518 he embarked on his epic series of frescoes for the Convent of San Paolo in Parma and followed this with the decoration of Parma Cathedral. He was the first Italian artist to paint the interior of a cupola, producing *The Ascension* for the church of San Giovanni in Parma. He also executed numerous religious and biblical paintings, but also occasionally drew on classical mythology for inspiration. His wife Girolama (b. 1504) is believed to have been his model for the *Madonna Reposing*, sometimes known as *Zingarella* ('Gipsy Girl').

MOVEMENT

Parma School

OTHER WORKS

Mystic Marriage of Saint Catherine; Ecce Homo

INFLUENCES

Leonardo da Vinci, Andrea Mantegna, Lorenzo Costa

Correggio *Born* 1494 Correggio, Italy

Died 1534

Holbein, Hans (after)

Henry VIII, c. 1540s

Courtesy of Private Collection/Christie's Images

Born at Augsburg, Germany, the son of Hans Holbein the Elder, Holbein studied under his father and then went to Basle with his brother Ambrosius as apprentice to Hans Herbst. Subsequently he worked also in Zurich and Lucerne. He returned to Basle in 1519, married and settled there. To his Swiss period belong his mostly religious works. In 1524 he went to France and thence to England in 1526, where he finally took up residence six years later. There being no demand for religious paintings in England at that time, he concentrated on portraiture, producing outstanding portraits of Sir Thomas More and Henry VIII, whose service he entered officially in 1537. From then until his death he produced numerous sensitive and lively studies of the King and his wives, his courtiers and high officials of state. He also designed stained-glass windows and executed woodcuts.

MOVEMENT

German School

OTHER WORKS

Dead Christ; The Triumphs of Wealth and Poverty,

INFLUENCES

Hans Holbein the Elder, Hans Herbst

Hans Holbein *Born* 1497 Augsburg, Germany

Died 1543

Titian (Tiziano Vecellio)

Venus and Adonis, 1555–60

Courtesy of Private Collection/Christie's Images

The greatest and most versatile artist of the Venetian Renaissance, Titian excelled equally at portraiture, religious pictures and mythological scenes. Born in the Dolomite region, he arrived in Venice as a boy and was apprenticed to a mosaicist. Turning to painting, he entered the studio of Giovanni Bellini, before joining forces with Giorgione. After Giorgione's premature death in 1510, Titian's star rose quickly. In 1511, he gained a major commission for frescoes in Padua, and in 1516 was appointed as the official painter of the Venetian Republic.

This honour enhanced Titian's international reputation and soon, offers of work began to flow in from the princely rulers of Ferrara, Urbino and Mantua. The painter did not always accept these commissions, as he was notoriously reluctant to travel, but some patrons could not be refused. The most distinguished of these was the Emperor Charles V. After their initial meeting in 1529, Titian was appointed Court Painter in 1533 and given the rank of Count Palatine. In 1548, he worked at the Imperial Court at Augsburg and his services were also prized by Charles's successor, Philip II.

MOVEMENT

Renaissance

OTHER WORKS

Bacchus and Ariadne; Man with a Glove; Sacred and Profane Love

INFLUENCES

Bellini, Giorgione

Titian *Born c.* 1485

Died 1576

Tintoretto

The Concert of Muses

Courtesy of Private Collection/Christie's Images

Born Jacopo Robusti, Tintoretto derived his nickname, meaning 'little dyer', from his father's trade. He was very briefly a pupil of Titian (who is said to have been jealous of the boy's talents) and though largely self-taught, was influenced by his master as well as Michelangelo and Sansovino. Apart from two trips to Mantua he spent his entire working life in Venice, painting religious subjects and contemporary portraits. His most ambitious project was the series of 50 paintings for the Church and School of San Rocco, but his fame rests on the spectacular *Paradise* (1588), a huge work crammed with figures. He was a master of dark tones illumined by adroit gleams of light. Three of his children became artists, including his daughter Marietta, known as La Tintoretta. His output was phenomenal and he painted with great rapidity and sureness of brushstrokes, earning him a second nickname of 'Il Furioso'.

MOVEMENT

Venetian School

OTHER WORKS

The Annunciation; The Last Supper; The Nine Muses

INFLUENCES

Michelangelo, Titian, Sansovino

Tintoretto *Born* 1518 Venice, Italy

Died 1594

Brueghel, Pieter

Hunters in the Snow, 1565

Also known as Brueghel the Elder to distinguish him from his son Pieter and younger son Jan, Pieter Brueghel was probably born about 1520 in the village of the same name near Breda. He studied under Pieter Coecke van Aelst (1502–50) and was greatly influenced by Hieronymous Bosch, from whom he developed his own peculiar style of late-medieval Gothic fantasy. About 1550 he travelled in France and Italy before returning to Brussels, where his most important paintings were executed. He was nicknamed 'Peasant Brueghel' from his custom of disguising himself in order to mingle with the peasants and beggars who formed the subjects of his rural paintings. Although he was a master of genre subjects his reputation rests mainly on his large and complex works, involving fantastic scenery and elaborate architecture, imbued with atmosphere and a sensitivity seldom achieved earlier.

MOVEMENT

Flemish School

OTHER WORKS

Tower of Babel; Peasant Wedding

INFLUENCES

Pieter Coecke, Hieronymus Bosch

Pieter Brueghel *Born c.* 1520 Brögel, Holland

Died 1569

Arcimboldo, Giuseppe

Winter, 1573

Courtesy of Kunsthistoriches Museum, Vienna/Bridgeman Art Library

Giuseppe Arcimboldo began his artistic career by working on the stained-glass windows in the Duomo (Cathedral) in Milan. Later he moved to Prague which, under Charles V, became for a time the centre of the Holy Roman Empire. Here he was employed by the Habsburg rulers as an architect (of the civic waterworks among other public projects), impresario of state occasions, curator of the imperial art collection and interior designer. It was in Prague that he painted the works on which his reputation now rests. In his exploration of human portraits composed of non-human and inanimate objects he was far ahead of his time, anticipating the Surrealists by several centuries. His fantastic heads symbolizing the four seasons were made up of pieces of landscape, flowers, vegetables and animals, even pots and pans and other mundane articles from everyday life, all executed in brilliant colours with an extraordinary attention to detail.

MOVEMENT

Surrealism

OTHER WORKS

Summer

INFLUENCES

Medieval stained glass

Giuseppe Arcimboldo *Born* 1527 Milan, Italy

Died 1593

da Caravaggio, Michelangelo Merisi
The Young Bacchus, c. 1591–93

Courtesy of Galleria Degli Uffizi, Florence/Bridgeman Art Library/Christie's Images

Born Michelangelo Merisi in the village of Caravaggio, Italy, Caravaggio studied in Milan and Venice before going to Rome to work under the patronage of Cardinal del Monte on altarpieces and religious paintings. His patron was startled not only by Caravaggio's scandalous behaviour but also by his rejection of the Roman ideals and techniques in painting. Instead, Caravaggio headed the *Naturalisti* (imitators of nature in the raw), developing a mastery of light and shade and concentrating on realism, regardless of theological correctness. As a result, some of his major commissions were rejected and in 1606, after he had killed a man in an argument, he fled from Rome to Naples and thence to Malta. On his return to Italy in 1609 he contracted a fever and died at Porto Ercole, Sicily. The years of exile produced one of his greatest portraits, the full-length *Grand Master of the Knights*.

MOVEMENT

Baroque

OTHER WORKS

Christ at Emmaus; The Card Players

INFLUENCES

Annibale Carracci

Caravaggio *Born c. 1572 Caravaggio, Italy*

Died 1610

The Age of Baroque & Rococo

1600–1770

Rubens, Peter Paul (attributed to)

Two Saints

Courtesy of Private Collection/Christie's Images

Born at Siegen, Westphalia, now part of Germany, Peter Paul Rubens was brought up in Antwerp in the Spanish Netherlands. Originally intended for the law, he studied painting under Tobias Verhaecht, Adam Van Noort and Otto Vaenius and was admitted into the Antwerp painters' guild in 1598. From 1600 to 1608 he was court painter to Vincenzo Gonzaga, Duke of Mantua, and travelled all over Italy and Spain, furthering his studies and also executing paintings for various churches. Shortly after his return to Antwerp he was appointed court painter to Archduke Albrecht of the Netherlands. In the last years of his life he combined painting with diplomatic missions which took him to France, Spain and England and resulted in many fine portraits, as well as his larger religious pieces. He was knighted by both Charles I and Philip IV of Spain. In 1630 he retired from the court to Steen and devoted the last years of his life to landscape painting.

MOVEMENT

Flemish School

OTHER WORKS

Samson and Delilah; The Descent from the Cross; Peace and War

INFLUENCES

Tobias Verhaecht, Adam Van Noort

Peter Paul Rubens *Born* 1577 Siegen, Germany

Died 1640

Poussin, Nicolas

The Triumph of David, c. 1631–3

Courtesy of Dulwich Picture Gallery, London, UK/Bridgeman Art Library

One of the leading exponents of Baroque painting, Nicolas Poussin settled in Paris in 1612. Ignoring the Mannerist painting then fashionable, he took Raphael as his model and studied the great Classical works of the Italian Renaissance. He left Paris in 1623 and began travelling in Italy, studying the works of the Italian masters at first hand. He settled in Rome the following year. Apart from a brief sojourn in Paris (1640–42) he spent the rest of his life in Rome, executing commissions for Cardinal Barberini. Eschewing the increasingly popular Baroque style, he clung to the Classical style and became its greatest French exponent. He drew upon the rich store of Greek and Roman mythology for his subjects, while utilizing the techniques of colour developed by Titian. His greatest canvasses deal with vast subjects, crowd scenes crammed with action and detail. Later on he tended to concentrate more on landscapes, although still steeped in the Classical tradition.

MOVEMENT

Classicism

OTHER WORKS

The Rape of the Sabines; The Worship of the Golden Calf

INFLUENCES

Raphael, Bernini

Nicolas Poussin *Born* 1594 Les Andelys, France

Died 1665

Guercino, II

Saint Luke

Courtesy of Private Collection/Christie's Images

Born Giovanni Francesco Barbieri, II Guercino is invariably known by his nickname, which means 'squint-eyed'. In spite of this handicap he showed early promise for sketching and drawing. He was trained in the rigorous classical mode at the Carracci Academy but was later influenced by the realism of Caravaggio, whose lighting techniques he modified by the richness of his colours. Like most artists of his generation he specialized in religious works — his major project being the fresco of *Aurora* which decorated the ceiling at the Villa Ludovisi, commissioned by Pope Gregory XV. From 1642 onwards he was the leading painter in Bologna, where he died. His oil paintings matched the rich density of their colours with the knack of conveying a wide range of emotions which heighten the dramatic impact of his work. There is invariably a dominant central figure, set against a background in the best Baroque tradition.

MOVEMENT

School of Bologna

OTHER WORKS

Jacob Receiving Joseph's Coat

INFLUENCES

Caravaggio

II Guercino *Born* 1602 Cento, Italy

Died 1666

van Dyck, Sir Anthony (circle of)
Self Portrait with a Sunflower, 1632

Courtesy of Private Collection/Philip Mould, Historical Portraits Ltd, London, UK/Bridgeman Art Library

Anthony van Dyck worked under Rubens and later travelled all over Italy, where he painted portraits and religious subjects. He first visited England in 1620 and was invited back in 1632 by King Charles I, who knighted him and appointed him Painter-in-Ordinary. Apart from a two-year period (1634–35) when he was back in Antwerp, van Dyck spent the rest of his life in England and on his return to London he embarked on the most prolific phase of his career. He not only painted numerous portraits of King Charles, Queen Henrietta Maria and their children, but also many pictures of courtiers and other notable figures, creating a veritable portrait gallery of the great and good of the period. His immense popularity was due not only to his technical mastery, but also his ability to give his sitters an expressiveness, grace and elegance, which few other artists have ever equalled.

MOVEMENT
Flemish School

OTHER WORKS
Charles I in Hunting Dress; The Three Royal Children

INFLUENCES
Peter Paul Rubens

Sir Anthony van Dyck *Born* 1599 Belgium
Died 1641

van Goyen, Jan

River Landscape with Lime Kilns, 1640s

Courtesy of Private Collection/Christie's Images

Jan van Goyen visited France in his youth and may have been influenced by the painters in that country, but he also travelled all over Holland and imbibed the ideas of his older contemporaries. With Salomon van Ruysdael he helped to establish the Dutch School of landscape painters and he had numerous pupils and imitators. In his travels he made countless sketches and drawings that formed the basis of his later oil paintings. He was a prolific artist but a poor businessman and died in debt. His landscapes divide into two periods, those dating from 1630 onwards being in more muted colours, predominantly shades of brown, but much more atmospheric. Towards the end of his life he began using a much greater range of colours again, coupled with that poetic sensibility which was the hallmark of the next generation of Dutch artists.

MOVEMENT

Dutch School

OTHER WORKS

A Castle by a River with Shipping at a Quay

INFLUENCES

Esaias van de Velde, Jan Porcellis

Jan van Goyen *Born* 1596 Leyden, Holland

Died 1656

Claesz, Pieter

A Vanitas Still Life, 1645

Courtesy of Johnny van Haeften Gallery, London, UK/Bridgeman Art Library

Born at Haarlem in the Netherlands in 1597 or 1598, Pieter Claesz grew up in a town which was the centre of the Dutch flower trade, so it was not surprising that he developed an early interest in floral painting. He grew up at a time when this style was being introduced to Holland by Flemish refugees, notably Ambrosius Bosschaert the Elder and Balthasar van der Alst. Claesz went on to develop the type of still life known as the breakfast or banquet picture – much less ebullient than the colourful flower paintings with more somber tones suited to the intimate atmosphere of domestic interiors. Claesz in fact took this further than his contemporaries, creating an almost monochrome effect and relying on the precise juxtaposition of each object which then took on a symbolic meaning. He pioneered a style that was emulated by many Dutch artists of the succeeding generation.

MOVEMENT

Dutch School

OTHER WORKS

Still Life with a Candle

INFLUENCES

Ambrosius Bosschaert, Balthasar van der Alst, Caravaggio

Pieter Claesz *Born c.* 1597 Haarlem, Holland

Died 1660

da Cortona, Pietro

Allegory of the Arts (ceiling painting)

Courtesy of Palazzo Barberini, Rome, Italy/Bridgeman Art Library

An Italian painter, architect, decorator, and designer, Pietro da Cortona was a versatile genius in the full Roman Baroque style. His first major works were frescos in Sta Bibiana, Rome, commissioned by Pope Urban VIII (Maffeo Barberini), and the patronage of the Barberini family played a major part in his career. For their palace he painted his most famous work, the huge ceiling fresco Allegory of Divine Providence. This was begun in 1633, but he interrupted the work in 1637 to go to Florence and paint two of four frescos commissioned by the Grand Duke of Tuscany for the Pitti Palace. He returned to finish the Barberini ceiling in 1639. This, one of the key works in the development of Baroque painting, is a triumph of illusionism, for the centre of the ceiling appears open to the sky and the figures seen from below appear to come down into the room as well as soar out of it. In 1640–47 Pietro returned to Florence to finish Pitti Palace frescos, where he received a new commission for seven ceilings, one of which is shown here.

MOVEMENT

Baroque

OTHER WORKS

The Triumph of Divine Providence (ceiling fresco)

INFLUENCES

Bernini

Pietro da Cortona *Born* 1596 Tuscany, Italy

Died 1669

de la Tour, Georges

The Newborn Child, late 1640s

Courtesy of Musee des Beaux-Arts, Rennes, France/Bridgeman Art Library

Born at Vic-sur-Seille, France, in 1593, Georges de la Tour established himself at Luneville about 1620, where he received many important commissions from the Duke of Lorraine. He also presented one of his paintings to King Louis XIII, who was so enchanted by it that he decided to remove paintings by all other artists from his private apartments. De la Tour concentrated on religious subjects, many of which were rather sombre with large areas of dark shadows and muted colours subtly illumined by a candle to create dark, dramatic and essentially realistic scenes. In this regard he was heavily influenced by Caravaggio and was, indeed, the leading French exponent of his particular brand of naturalism, although eschewing Caravaggio's penchant for the macabre. De la Tour's paintings exude serenity in keeping with their subject matter. Like his paintings, however, he languished in obscurity for many years and was not rediscovered until 1915.

MOVEMENT

French School

OTHER WORKS

St Peter Denying Christ

INFLUENCES

Caravaggio

Georges de la Tour *Born* 1593 France

Died 1652

Hals, Frans

Portrait of a Gentleman, c. 1650–52

Born at Antwerp about 1580, Frans Hals moved with his family to Haarlem at an early age and spent the whole of his life there. It is believed that he received his earliest instruction from Adam Van Noort in Antwerp but continued his studies under Van Mander. None of his earliest works appears to have survived, but from 1618 onwards, when he painted *Two Boys Playing* and *Arquebusiers of St George*, his works show great technical mastery allied to that spirit and passion which made him the equal of Rembrandt in portraiture. His most famous work, *The Laughing Cavalier* is universally recognized, but it is only one of many expressive portraits, distinguished by a liveliness that was far ahead of its time and anticipating the work of the Impressionists. After 1640 his work mellowed and he adopted a darker and more contemplative style.

MOVEMENT

Dutch School

OTHER WORKS

Man with a Cane; Regents of the Company of St Elisabeth

INFLUENCES

Van Noort, Van Mander

Frans Hals *Born c. 1580 Antwerp, Holland*

Died 1666

Shouping, Yun

Lotus Flower

Courtesy of Osaka Museum of Fine Arts, Japan/Bridgeman Art Library

A notable poet and calligrapher, Yun Shouping was second only to Wu Li among the Chinese painters who were neither orthodox nor individualist, and therefore he does not fit into any exact category. He has often been dismissed merely as a flower painter, but this does not do justice to his art as a landscape painter. Of course, more than any other artist of his period, he loved to decorate his pictures with masses of flowers, but this does not detract from the fact that his landscapes themselves are among the most serenely beautiful and perfect productions among the later Chinese artists. In his studies of flowers and plants as such, however, he was unsurpassed for the delicacy and clarity of his draughtsmanship and the care he took with his compositions. He preferred a very wet brush so that the ink flowed freely, producing a very sharp, clean-cut line. His landscape paintings are very similar to those of the four Wangs and Wu Li, but it is in his use of floral ornament that he stands out from his contemporaries.

MOVEMENT

Early Ming Period

OTHER WORKS

Bamboo and Old Tree; Peonies; Plum Blossoms

INFLUENCES

Wang Yuanqi, Wang Hui, Wu Li

Yun Shouping *Born* 1633 Wujin, Jiangsu, China

Died 1690

Cuyp, Albert

The Maas at Dordrecht with Fishing Boats

Courtesy of Private Collection/Christie's Images

Albert Cuyp, or Cuijp, was the son of the painter Jacob Gerritsz Cuyp (1594–*c.* 1652), scion of a well-to-do family. Controversy continues to rage over the extent of his work, many paintings, particularly of still life, being merely signed with the initials AC. On the other hand, those paintings signed 'A Cuyp' are generally landscapes, whose startling lighting effects are very characteristic of his work. As the signed canvasses belong to his later period, it has been argued that the AC paintings are from his earliest years as a painter. He never strayed beyond the Netherlands and his landscapes are bounded by the Maas and the Rhine, but what the flatness of the scenery lacks in variety is more than compensated for by Cuyp's mastery of conveying the different seasons and even different times of day, at their best suffusing the figures of humans and animals with brilliant sunshine.

MOVEMENT

Dutch School

OTHER WORKS

Dordrecht Evening; Cattle with Horseman and Peasants

INFLUENCES

Van Goyen and Jan Both

Albert Cuyp *Born* 1620 Dordrecht, Holland

Died 1691

de Hooch, Pieter

The Courtyard of a House in Delft, 1658

Pieter de Hooch spent his early life in Rotterdam but when he married in 1654 he settled in Delft. Here he came under the influence of Carel Fabritius shortly before the latter's untimely death in the explosion of the Delft Arsenal. De Hooch was subsequently influenced by the late artist's gifted pupil Jan Vermeer. De Hooch himself became one of the leading masters of paintings showing domestic interiors or courtyard scenes, with the emphasis on order, domestic virtue, cleanliness to the point of ascetism and benign tranquillity, shown through the careful arrangement of furniture and figures. His pictures are characterized by a dark foreground, often a doorway or gateway, leading to a bright interior suffused with light and colour. He was an accomplished technician, noted for his complete mastery of perspective which enabled him to create an almost three-dimensional effect.

MOVEMENT

Dutch School

OTHER WORKS

Woman and a Maid with a Pail in a Courtyard

INFLUENCES

Carel Fabritius, Vermeer

Pieter de Hooch *Born* 1629 Rotterdam, Holland

Died 1684

Rembrandt, Harmensz van Rijn
Self Portrait, 1658

One of Holland's greatest and most versatile artists, Rembrandt trained under several painters, the most influential of these being Pieter Lastman. For a time he shared a studio with Jan Lievens, but by the early 1630s he had moved to Amsterdam, where he established a formidable reputation as a portraitist. Rembrandt's approach to group portraiture, in particular, was extremely ambitious. He showed the anatomist, Dr Tulp actually performing a dissection, while his most famous canvas, *The Night Watch*, is a stunningly complex composition portraying a local militia group.

As the 1640s progressed, Rembrandt's art entered a more reflective phase. He painted fewer fashionable portraits, preferring instead to depict the inner life. This can be seen in his magnificent religious paintings, in his intimate, unidealized portrayals of his two wives, Saskia and Hendrickje, and in a penetrating series of self-portraits – perhaps the finest ever produced by any artist. Rembrandt's later work was less commercially successful and, although this led to insolvency, the popular image of him as a reclusive pauper is entirely fictitious.

MOVEMENT

Baroque

OTHER WORKS

The Night Watch; The Anatomy Lesson of Dr. Tulp; The Jewish Bride

INFLUENCES

Pieter Lastman, Jan Lievens, Rubens

Rembrandt *Born* 1606 Leiden, Holland

Died 1669

Hobbema, Meindert

A River Landscape with a Ruined Building and Figures, c. 1660s

Courtesy of Private Collection/Christie's Images

Originally named Meindert Lubbertszoon, Hobbema studied under Jacob van Ruysdael in his native city. They were close friends and often painted the same subjects; as Hobbema lacked his master's genius in raising the dramatic temperature in his landscapes, Hobbema languished in his shadow. This must also have been the attitude of the picture-buying public at the time, for eventually Hobbema was obliged to forsake painting and work as an excise man, an arduous occupation that left him little time or inclination for art. While it is true that many of his paintings are not particularly distinguished, Hobbema at his best could be sublime and in recent times his painting has been the subject of considerable re-appraisal. It is generally recognized that his greatest achievement was *The Avenue, Middelharnis* – deceptively simple, yet a painting of immense subtlety and complex detail.

MOVEMENT

Dutch School

OTHER WORKS

Stormy Landscape; Road on a Dyke; Watermill with a Red Roof

INFLUENCES

Jacob and Salomon van Ruysdael

Meindert Hobbema *Born* 1638 Amsterdam, Holland

Died 1709

Cooper, Samuel

Miniature of James II as the Duke of York, 1661

Courtesy of Victoria & Albert Museum, London, UK/Bridgeman Art Library

Samuel Cooper is often regarded as the greatest painter of miniatures who ever lived; certainly he was instrumental in raising the status of miniature painting to new heights. He learned his skills from his uncle, John Hoskins. Pepys mentions Cooper frequently in his diaries and noted that he was a fine musician and a good linguist in addition to his artistic talents. He lived through turbulent times and had the distinction of holding official appointments both under the Commonwealth and later the Crown following the Restoration of 1660. He painted several portraits of both Oliver Cromwell and King Charles II, including the effigy of the King used for the coinage. As well as miniatures, painted on ivory or fine parchment, he was also a prolific draughtsman, his collection of chalk drawings being preserved in the University Gallery, Oxford.

MOVEMENT

English Miniaturists

OTHER WORKS

John Aubrey; Mrs Pepys; Self Portrait

INFLUENCES

John Hoskins

Samuel Cooper *Born* 1609 London, England

Died 1672

van Ruysdael, Salomon

A Wooded Landscape with Cattle and Drovers on a Ferry, 1663

Courtesy of Private Collection/Christie's Images

Born at Naarden in Gooiland, Salomon Jacobsz van Ruysdael was originally Salomon de Gooyer, but he and his brother Isaack (1599–77) adopted the name 'Ruysdael' from a castle near their father's home. Salomon joined the Painters' Guild at Haarlem in 1623, becoming Dean in 1648. From 1651 he also had a business supplying blue dyes to the Haarlem bleachworks. His earliest dated works belong to 1626 and within two years of this his reputation as a landscape painter was assured. Although he remained in Haarlem all his life, he made occasional forays to other parts of the Netherlands in search of landscape subjects, noted for their fine tonal qualities, and laying the foundations for the great paintings of his much more famous nephew Jacob van Ruysdael. As well as his tranquil landscapes and river scenes, he produced a number of still-life paintings towards the end of his career.

MOVEMENT

Dutch School

OTHER WORKS

Utrecht; Still Life

INFLUENCES

Esaias van de Velde, Jan van Goyen

Salomon van Ruysdael *Born c. 1600 Holland*

Died 1670

Vermeer, Jan

Girl with a Pearl Earring, c. 1665–6

Courtesy of Mauritshuis, The Hague, Netherlands/Bridgeman Art Library

Jan Vermeer studied painting under Carel Fabritius. In 1653 he entered the Guild of St Luke taking the role of head there in 1662 and 1670. Diffident and a poor businessman, he died young, leaving a widow and eight children destitute. He was almost entirely forgotten until 1860, when he was rediscovered and works which had previously been attributed to other artists were properly identified as coming from his brush. He specialized in small paintings of domestic scenes, distinguished by their perspective and clever use of light to create subtle tones, as well as the fact that, unusual for the time, the figures in them are self-absorbed. Only about 40 paintings have definitely been credited to him, but they are sufficient to establish him as one of the more original and innovative painters of his time – second only to Rembrandt.

MOVEMENT

Dutch School

OTHER WORKS

Lady Seated at a Virginal; The Painter in his Studio; View of Delft

INFLUENCES

Carel Fabritius

Jan Vermeer *Born* 1632 Delft, Holland

Died 1675

Pozzo, Andrea

The Entry of Saint Ignatius Into Paradise, c. 1707

Courtesy of Church of St Ignatius, Rome, Italy/Bridgeman Art Library

One of the most brilliant painters and architects of his generation, Andrea Pozzo was the pupil of an unknown master whom he accompanied to Milan, where he became a Jesuit lay brother. In this connection he was responsible for the decorations of religious festivals and from this graduated to theatrical sets. In 1676 he painted the frescoes for the church of San Francisco Saverio in Modovi, a masterpiece of trompe l'oeil. This was a foretaste of his greatest illusionistic masterpiece, the ceiling of the church of St Ignatius in Rome which, by an ingenious use of perspective, appears to expand the interior by hundreds of feet. In this immense achievement he united his talents as painter, architect and sculptor to great effect. In 1695 he designed the elaborate tomb of Ignatius Loyola, founder of the Society of Jesus. He worked on the decoration of many other churches in Italy and from 1703 onwards was similarly employed in Vienna.

MOVEMENT

Italian Baroque

OTHER WORKS

St Francis Xavier Preaching; Investiture of St Francesco Borgia

INFLUENCES

Andrea Sacchi, Pietro da Cortona, Bernini

Andrea Pozzo *Born* 1642 Trento, Italy

Died 1709

Watteau, Jean-Antoine

Les Plaisir du Bal ('The Pleasures of a Ball'), c. 1714

Jean-Antoine Watteau studied under Gérin but learned more from the paintings of Ostade and Teniers. On his master's death, Watteau went to Paris, where he worked for the scene-painter Métayer and then in a factory where he turned out cheap religious pictures by the dozen. He was rescued from this drudgery by Claude Gillot and later worked under Claude Audran. The turning point came when he won second prize in a Prix de Rome competition in 1709. He became an associate of the Academy in 1712 and a full member in 1717. He led the revolt against the pompous classicism of the Louis XIV period and broke new ground with his realism and lively imagination. His early works were mainly military subjects, but later he concentrated on rustic idylls which were very fashionable in the early eighteenth century.

MOVEMENT

French School

OTHER WORKS

The Music Party; Embarkation for the Isle of Cythera

INFLUENCES

Claude Audran, David Teniers

Jean-Antoine Watteau *Born* 1684 France

Died 1721

Carriera, Rosalba

Portrait of Prince Charles Edward Stuart

Courtesy of Private Collection/Christie's Images

The daughter of the painter Andrea Carriera, Rosalba was taught by her father and worked in pastels and oils. She painted mostly miniature portraits in oils on ivory both for framing and mounting in snuff-boxes, but by the beginning of the eighteenth century she had diversified into larger portraits mainly executed in pastels. Soon gaining a high reputation in this medium, she was admitted to the Academy of St Luke at Rome in 1705. As well as formal portraits she painted genre subjects, mainly dealing with the everyday lives of women, latterly she also painted allegorical scenes and figures from classical mythology. Her style matured significantly from about 1711, and her portraits became much more expressive of the sitter's character. In 1720–22 she worked in Paris and was admitted to membership of the Académie Royale. From 1723 onwards she was much in demand at the courts of Europe to paint royal portraits.

MOVEMENT

Venetian School

OTHER WORKS

Antoine Watteau; Empress Amalia; Lady Cutting her Hair

INFLUENCES

Andrea Carriera, Federico Bencovich, Giovanni Pellegrini

Rosalba Carriera *Born* 1675 Venice, Italy

Died 1757

Hogarth, William

The Beggars' Opera, 1728–31

Courtesy of Private Collection/Christie's Images

William Hogarth became the greatest English satirical artist of his generation. He was apprenticed to a silver-plate engraver, Ellis Gamble, and established his own business in 1720. Seeking to diversify into the more lucrative business of copper-plate engraving, however he took lessons in draughtsmanship under Sir James Thornhill. His early work consisted mainly of ornamental bill-heads and business cards, but by 1724 he was designing plates for booksellers and from this he progressed to individual prints, before turning to portrait painting by 1730. Within a few years he had begun to concentrate on the great satirical works on which his reputation now rests. His canvasses are absolutely crammed with figures and minute detail, sub-plots and side issues to the main theme. Following a visit to Paris in 1743 he produced several prints of low life and moral subjects. He also executed a number of portraits and oils of genre subjects.

MOVEMENT

English School

OTHER WORKS

Marriage à la Mode; Industry and Idleness; Garrick as Richard III

INFLUENCES

Sir James Thornhill

William Hogarth *Born* 1697 London, England

Died 1764

Chardin, Jean-Baptiste-Siméon

Still Life with Ray and Basket of Onions, 1731

A French painter, specializing in still life and genre scenes, Chardin was born in Paris where he spent most of his life. His father was a carpenter and, initially, he seemed destined to follow this trade, until his aptitude for painting became apparent. As a youth, Chardin trained under two very minor history painters, Pierre Cazes and Noel-Nicolas Coypel, but his real education came from copying Dutch and Flemish paintings in private art collections. These prompted him to concentrate on still-life pictures – a brave decision, since this type of painting had a low reputation and was very poorly paid. Despite these drawbacks, Chardin's career flourished. In 1728, *The Skate* won such acclaim at a Paris exhibition that he was invited to become a full member of the Academy, an unprecedented honour for a still life artist. Chardin was delighted and became a stalwart of the institution, holding the post of Treasurer for 20 years. Even so, he found it hard to make a living and, accordingly, extended his repertoire to include simple domestic scenes. These wonderful vignettes of everyday life displayed none of the affectation of the prevailing Rococo style and proved enormously popular with the public.

MOVEMENT

Still life and genre

OTHER WORKS

Saying Grace, The Brioche

INFLUENCES

Nicolaes Maes; Jean-Baptiste Oudry

Jean-Baptiste-Siméon Chardin *Born* 1699 Paris, France

Died 1779

Canaletto

Grand Canal, c. 1740

Courtesy of Private Collection/Christie's Images

Originally named Giovanni Antonio Canale, Canaletto was the son of a scene-painter in whose footsteps he at first followed. In 1719 he went to Rome to study architecture and on his return to Venice he began painting those great architectural masterpieces with which he has been associated ever since. Although most of his paintings illustrate the buildings and canals of his native city – executed as souvenirs for wealthy patrons from England making the Grand Tour – he lived mainly in London from 1746 to 1753. This is reflected in his paintings of the Thames and the City, and other views in the Home Counties. He then returned to Venice where he became a member of the Academy in 1763. He established a style of architectural painting that was widely imitated by the next generation of Italian artists, notably Francesco Guardi and his own nephew Bernardo Bellotto, who slavishly imitated him and even signed his works 'Canaletto'.

MOVEMENT

Venetian School

OTHER WORKS

Piazza San Marco; Regatta on the Grand Canal

INFLUENCES

Tiepolo

Canaletto *Born* 1697 Venice, Italy

Died 1768

Boucher, François (attributed to)
La Cible d'Amour ('The Target of Love'), 1758

Courtesy of Private Collection/Christie's Images

A French painter and designer, Boucher was one of the greatest masters of the Rococo style. Born in Paris, Boucher was the son of a versatile, not particularly successful, artist and craftsman. As a result, he learned a wide variety of artistic techniques in his father's workshop before training more formally under François Lemoyne. Boucher's first significant job was to produce a set of engravings after Watteau's drawings, but he also found time to paint, winning the Prix de Rome in 1723. After making the traditional study-tour of Italy (1727–31), he began to gain official plaudits for his work. In 1735 he was granted his first royal commission and this secured his position as a court artist. This role governed the nature of Boucher's art. There were no grand, intellectual themes or moral dramas in his pictures. Instead, he painted light-hearted mythologies and pastoral idylls, which could serve equally well as paintings, tapestry designs or porcelain decoration. This is also evident in Boucher's work for his most distinguished patron, Madame de Pompadour. He immortalized her in a series of dazzling portraits, but also decorated her palace and designed sets for her private theatre.

MOVEMENT

Rococo

OTHER WORKS

The Triumph of Venus; Mademoiselle O'Murphy

INFLUENCES

Watteau, Abraham Bloemaert, François Lemoyne

François Boucher *Born* 1703, Paris

Died 1770

Fragonard, Jean-Honoré

Les Hazards Heureux de l'Escarpolette

('The Swing'), 1767

Courtesy of Wallace Collection, London, UK/Bridgeman Art Library

A leading exponent of the light-hearted Rococo style, Fragonard trained under Boucher (Madame de Pompadour's favourite artist) and won the Prix de Rome, both of which seemed to mark him out for a conventional career as a history painter. But he was too ill-disciplined to enjoy the business of copying old masters and his studies in Rome (1756–60) did not progress well. Instead, the Italian countryside awakened Fragonard's interest in landscape painting while, on his return to France, the success of *The Swing* led his art in a different direction. The painting demonstrated Fragonard's undoubted gift for playful eroticism, and it brought him a series of commissions for similar 'boudoir' pictures. Patrons were attracted by his dazzling, vivacious style and by his innate sense of taste, which strayed close to the margins of decency, but never crossed them. In this sense, Fragonard became the archetypal painter of the Ancien Régime and ultimately shared its fate. By the 1780s, Neoclassicism had all but supplanted the Rococo style and, although he received help from David after the Revolution in 1789, Fragonard's later years were marred by poverty and neglect.

MOVEMENT

Rococo

OTHER WORKS

The Progress of Love; The Bolt; The Love Letter

INFLUENCES

François Boucher, Hubert Robert, Tiepolo

Jean-Honoré Fragonard *Born* 1732, France

Died 1806

Gainsborough, Thomas

Portrait of David Garrick, exhibited 1770

Born in Sudbury, Suffolk Gainsborough displayed precocious artistic skills. According to family legend, he helped catch a pear thief in a neighbour's orchard by accurately sketching the culprit. Recognizing his obvious talent, his family sent him to London at the age of 13, where he was trained by the French Rococo artist Hubert Gravelot. In 1745, Gainsborough set up in business hoping to make a living selling landscapes, but the venture failed and he returned to Suffolk. Gainsborough preferred landscapes to 'face-painting', but found that portraiture was far more profitable. With this in mind, he eventually moved from Suffolk to the fashionable resort of Bath, where he was employed by a rich and illustrious clientele. Here, Gainsborough honed his skills to perfection, often painting by candlelight, in order to give his brushwork its distinctive, flickering appearance. By 1768, he was so famous that he was invited to become one of the founder members of the Royal Academy. Gainsborough accepted, and spent the final years of his career in London vying with Reynolds for supremacy in the field of portraiture.

MOVEMENT

Rococo

OTHER WORKS

The Morning Walk; The Painter's Daughters Chasing a Butterfly

INFLUENCES

Hubert Gravelot, Van Dyck, Francis Hayman

Thomas Gainsborough *Born* 1727 England

Died 1788

The Age of Neoclassicism & Romanticism

1760–1860

Reynolds, Sir Joshua

George Townshend

Courtesy of Private Collection/Christie's Images

Born in Plympton, Devon, Joshua Reynolds was apprenticed in London to Thomas Hudson, a second-rate portrait painter from whom he learned the rudiments of his craft. In 1743 Reynolds settled in Plymouth, but in 1744 he returned to London, where his portrait of Captain John Hamilton brought him recognition. Reynolds spent two years in Rome perfecting his technique, then visited other Italian art centres before returning to England in 1752. By 1760 he was the most fashionable portrait painter in London, becoming the first President of the Royal Academy in 1768 and knighted a year later. A prolific artist, he produced over 2,000 portraits, many of which were subsequently published as engravings that further enhanced his reputation.

MOVEMENT

English School

OTHER WORKS

Nelly O'Brien; Samuel Johnson

INFLUENCES

Thomas Hudson, Sir Peter Lely

Sir Joshua Reynolds *Born* 1723 England

Died 1792

Fuseli, Henry

The Nightmare, 1781

This compelling image is one of the key works of the Romantic movement, combining the themes of mystery, horror and tortured sexuality. A young woman lies unconscious with her head dangling uncomfortably over the edge of the bed. She is in the grip of a terrible nightmare, inflicted on her by an incubus that squats on the pit of her stomach. On the left, the head of a spectral horse peers round from behind a curtain. This is the 'night-mare', the terrible creature that transports the incubus on his nocturnal visitations.

In the Middle Ages the incubus was defined as a demon lover, who assumed human form and preyed on young women by night. The female equivalent was the succubus, who sought out male victims. The incubus could impregnate its partners. In some tales, Merlin is said to have been fathered by an incubus. Equally the parents of some illegitimate children, including a number of medieval nuns, ascribed their unexpected pregnancy to rape by an incubus. The 'night-mare' took its name from Mara or Mera, another demon. Fuseli painted several other, less potent, versions of the subject, usually showing the incubus galloping away from the bedroom of one of his victims.

MOVEMENT

Romanticism

SIMILAR WORKS

Milton's Mysterious Dream by William Blake

MEDIUM

Oil on canvas

Henry Fuseli *Born* 1741 Switzerland

Died 1825

Romney, George
Portrait of Emma, Lady Hamilton, 1786

Courtesy of Philip Mould, Historical Portraits Ltd, London, UK/Bridgeman Art Library

An English painter specializing in portraits, Romney was born in Lancashire, the son of a cabinet maker, and trained under an itinerant portraitist named Christopher Steele. For a time, he picked up commissions by travelling from town to town, before making his base in Kendal. Moving to London in 1762, he established a reputation as a fashionable portrait painter, although his style did not really mature until after his tour of Italy (1773–75). There, his study of Classical and Renaissance art paid huge dividends and most of his best paintings were produced in the decade after his return to England.

Romney, like Gainsborough, was deeply dissatisfied with portraiture. His ambition of becoming a history painter was never fulfilled, perhaps partly because of his nervous, introspective character and partly because of his reluctance to exhibit. His later career was marred by his obsession with Emma Hart, later to become Lady Hamilton and Nelson's mistress. Romney met her in 1781, and in the years that followed produced dozens of pictures of her, usually masquerading as a character from mythology. As his reputation began to wane, the artist returned to Kendal, where he suffered a serious mental decline.

MOVEMENTS

Neoclassicism, Romanticism

OTHER WORKS

The Parson's Daughter; The Beaumont Family; Lady Rodbard

INFLUENCES

Sir Joshua Reynolds, Henry Fuseli, Joseph Highmore

George Romney *Born 1734 England*

Died 1802

Vigée-Lebrun, (Marie Louise) Elisabeth

Marie Antoinette and her Four Children, 1787

Courtesy of Chateau de Versailles, France/Bridgeman Art Library

Marie Louise Elisabeth Vigée-Lebrun was the daughter of an artist from whom she received her early training, but later benefited from the help of several fellow-painters. By the age of 20 she had already made her mark with portraits of Count Orloff and the Duchess of Orleans. In 1783 she was admitted to the Academy on the strength of her allegorical masterpiece *Peace Bringing Back Abundance*. Following the outbreak of the Revolution she fled to Italy and worked in Rome and Naples, later visiting Vienna, Berlin and St Petersburg. She returned briefly to Paris in 1802 but went to London the same year, where she painted the Prince of Wales and Lord Byron. She was a prolific portraitist and a score of her paintings portray Marie Antoinette alone.

MOVEMENT

French School

OTHER WORKS

Portrait of the Artist and her Daughter

INFLUENCES

Joseph Vernet, Jean Baptiste Grueze, Charles Lebrun

Elisabeth Vigée-Lebrun *Born* 1755 France

Died 1842

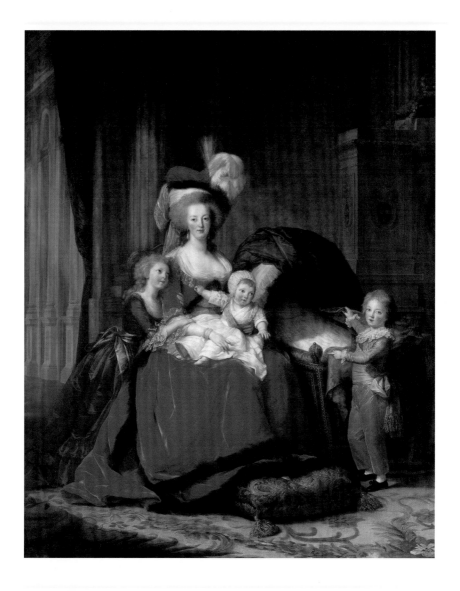

Girtin, Thomas

Dunstanborough Castle, c. 1797

Courtesy of Private Collection/Christie's Images

Thomas Girtin served his apprenticeship in London as a mezzotint engraver under Edward Dayes, through whom he made the acquaintance of J. M. W. Turner who, being shown Girtin's architectural and topographical sketches, encouraged him to develop his talents as a landscape painter. His early death in 1802 from tuberculosis brought a very promising career to an untimely end, but even by then he had established a high reputation as an etcher. Hitherto, watercolours had been used almost entirely for tinting engravings, but to Girtin goes the credit for establishing watercolour painting as a major art form in its own right. From 1794 onwards he exhibited his great watercolour landscapes at the annual Royal Academy exhibitions and this helped to develop the fashion for this medium from the beginning of the nineteenth century. Girtin collaborated with Turner in making a series of copies of architectural paintings for Dr Monro, notably works by Canaletto.

MOVEMENT

English School

OTHER WORKS

A Winding Estuary; Porte St Denis

INFLUENCES

Turner

Thomas Girtin *Born* 1775 London, England

Died 1802

Gros, Antoine-Jean

Napoleon Bonaparte Visiting the Plague Stricken of Jaffa, 1799

Courtesy of Louvre, Paris, France/Bridgeman Art Library

The son of a miniature painter, Antoine-Jean Gros studied under Jacques-Louis David. Following the death of his father in 1791 he went to Italy and it was there that he met Josephine Beauharnais, who introduced him to Napoleon, whom he accompanied on his Italian campaign. He was an eye-witness of the dramatic scene when Bonaparte planted the Tricolour on the bridge at Arcole in November 1796 and the dramatic painting that recorded this incident gave Gros a sense of purpose. Thereafter, as a war artist, he chronicled on canvas the exploits of the Napoleonic army down to the campaign of 1811, and it is on these heroic paintings that his reputation is largely based, earning him the Napoleonic title of Baron in the process. The downfall of Napoleon robbed Gros of his true vocation. In the aftermath of Waterloo he returned to his classicist roots and concentrated on such works as *Hercules and Diomedes*, but by now he was fighting a losing battle against the rising tide of Romanticism.

MOVEMENT

French Classicism

OTHER WORKS

The Departure of Louis XVIII

INFLUENCES

David

Antoine-Jean Gros *Born* 1771 Paris, France

Died 1835

Goya, Francisco

The Clothed Maja, c. 1800–05

Courtesy of Prado, Madrid, Bridgeman Art Library/Christie's Images

Francisco José de Goya y Lucientes was raised in the small town of Fuendetodos near Saragossa, Spain. Frequently involved in parochial gang fights, he fled to Madrid in 1765 after a brawl in which three youths were killed. As a result of continued sparring he left Madrid precipitately, joining a troupe of itinerant bull-fighters and eventually reaching Rome, where he resumed his studies in art. In 1798 he returned to Spain as a designer for the royal tapestry factory and executed a number of frescoes drawn from contemporary life, as well as a series of satirical etchings. In 1799 he was appointed court painter to Charles IV, which resulted in some of his most notable portraits. After the French invasion in 1808 he sided at first with the invaders, but secretly sketched their atrocities, which resulted in both full-scale canvasses and numerous etchings. In 1824 he moved to Bordeaux where, in old age, he produced some of his finest genre paintings.

MOVEMENT

Spanish School

OTHER WORKS

Execution of the Defenders of Madrid; The Naked Maja

INFLUENCES

Anton Raphael Mengs, Tiepolo

Francisco Goya *Born* 1746 Fuendetodos, Spain

Died 1828

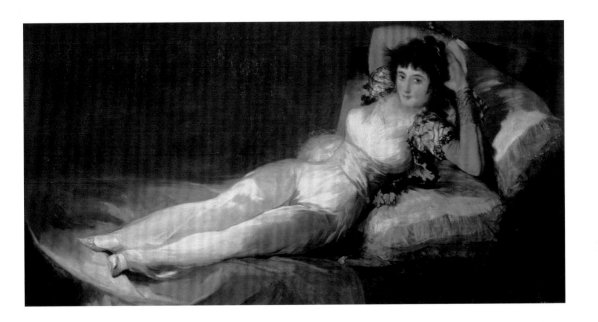

Constable, John

Lock on the Stour

Constable was a pioneering British artist who, together with Turner, raised the status of landscape painting in England. He enjoyed a happy childhood in his native Suffolk and this region became the focus for most of his paintings. In Constable's day, however, landscape painting was a poorly paid profession and both his family and that of his lover, Maria Bicknell, were appalled by his choice of career. For many years, the couple were forced to meet in secret, until they eventually married in 1816. Constable's struggle for success was as difficult as his father had feared and, for a time, he was obliged to paint portraits for a living. In part, this was because he did not seek out romantic or picturesque views, but preferred to paint his local area, even though many regarded it as dull, agricultural land. He also paid unprecedented attention to atmospheric conditions, making copious sketches of individual clouds. These were so realistic that one critic joked that Constable's paintings always made him want to reach for his umbrella. Eventually, he found success with his 'six-footers' (i.e. six feet wide), gaining membership of the Royal Academy and winning a gold medal at the Paris Salon.

MOVEMENT

Romanticism

OTHER WORKS

The Hay Wain; Flatford Mill; Salisbury Cathedral

INFLUENCES

Thomas Gainsborough, Jacob van Ruisdael, Claude Lorrain

John Constable *Born* 1776, Suffolk, England

Died 1837

Ingres, Jean-Auguste-Dominique

Jupiter and Thetis, 1811

Courtesy of Private Collection/Christie's Images

A French painter and draughtsman, Ingres was a champion of academic art. Ingres' father was a minor painter and sculptor and, with parental encouragement, he displayed a talent for both drawing and music at a very early age. Opting for the former, he moved to Paris in 1797 and entered David's studio. There, inspired by his teacher and by Flaxman's engravings of antique vases, Ingres developed a meticulous Neo-classical style, notable for impeccable draughtsmanship and a smooth, enamel-like finish. This helped him to win the Prix de Rome in 1801 and brought him a succession of lucrative portrait commissions.

Ingres worked extensively in Italy after 1806, although he continued to exhibit at the Salon and rapidly became the epitome of the academic establishment. This was most obvious in the 1820s, when his pictures were contrasted with those of Delacroix, in the 'battle' between Classicism and Romanticism. While his style was a model of classical correctness, however, Ingres' subject matter was often distinctly Romantic. This is particularly evident in the exotic eroticism of Oriental scenes, such as *La Grande Odalisque* and *The Turkish Bath*.

MOVEMENT

Neoclassicism, Romanticism

OTHER WORKS

Madame Moitessier; The Apotheosis of Homer

INFLUENCES

David, Raphael, John Flaxman

Jean-Auguste-Dominique Ingres *Born* 1780

Died 1867

Cotman, John Sell

Fishing Boats off Yarmouth

Courtesy of Christie's Images/Bridgeman Art Library

John Sell Cotman received his art training in London before returning to his native Norwich in 1806, where he became the foremost watercolourist among the group of East Anglian artists who came to be known as the Norwich School. In the early years of the nineteenth century he travelled extensively in England and Wales and his best work belongs to this period. Although chiefly remembered for his work in this medium he also executed a number of fine oil paintings during the time he resided at Great Yarmouth from 1811–23. Failing in business, however, he was forced to sell all his paintings and etchings and return to London, where he obtained a position as drawing master at King's College. There is an uncompromisingly austere character to his landscapes, very much ahead of his time and not at all in step with the fashions prevailing in Regency England, but his handling of light and shade was to have a profound influence on his followers.

MOVEMENT

English Landscape School

OTHER WORKS

Greta Bridge; Chirk Aqueduct; Duncombe Park

INFLUENCES

Thomas Girtin, Turner

John Sell Cotman *Born* 1782, Norfolk, England

Died 1842

Friedrich, Caspar David

The Wanderer Above the Sea of Clouds, 1818

Courtesy of Hamburg Kunsthalle, Hamburg, Germany/Bridgeman Art Library

Caspar David Friedrich studied drawing under J. G. Quistorp in Greifswald before going to the Copenhagen Academy between 1794–98. On his return to Germany he settled in Dresden, where he spent the rest of his life. His drawings in pen and ink were admired by Goethe and won him a Weimar Art Society prize in 1805. His first major commission came two years later in the form of an altarpiece for Count Thun's castle in Teschen, Silesia, entitled *Crucifixion in Mountain Scenery*. This set the tone of many later works, in which dramatic landscapes expressed moods, emotions and atmosphere. Appointed a professor of the Dresden Academy in 1824, he influenced many of the young German and Scandinavian artists of the mid-nineteenth century and as a result he ranks high among the formative figures of the Romantic movement. For many years his works were neglected, but in the early 1900s they were rediscovered and revived.

MOVEMENT

Romanticism

OTHER WORKS

The Wreck of the Hope; The Stages of Life; Graveyard in Snow

INFLUENCES

Albrecht Altdorfer, Turner

Caspar David Friedrich *Born* 1774 Germany

Died 1840

Géricault, Théodore

Homme Nu a Mi-Corps ('Man Naked to the Waist')

Jean Louis André Théodore Géricault studied under Carle Vernet and Pierre Narcisse Guérin, although he was frequently at odds with the latter because of his passion for Rubens and his unconventional approach in interpreting nature. He made his debut at the Salon of 1812 with his spirited portrait of a cavalry officer on horseback, and followed this with the *Wounded Cuirassier* in 1814, subjects which were immensely popular at the height of the Napoleonic Empire. During the Hundred Days, he served as a volunteer in a Royalist regiment, witnessing soldiers and horses at close quarters. He travelled and studied in Italy from 1816–19, and on his return to Paris embarked on the large-scale works which established his reputation as one of the leading French Romantics. For an artist renowned for his equestrian subjects it is ironic that he died as the result of a fall from his horse.

MOVEMENT

Romanticism

OTHER WORKS

Officer of the Hussars; Coirse des Chevaux Libres

INFLUENCES

Carle Vernet, Pierre Narcisse Guérin

Théodore Géricault *Born* 1791 Rouen, France

Died 1824

Hokusai, Katsushika

In the Well of the Great Wave, 1823-29

Courtesy of Private Collection/Christie's Images

Born at Edo (now Tokyo), the son of a mirror maker, Hokusai learned the craft of wood-engraving before entering the studio of the painter Katsugawa Shunsho. Disagreement with his master over artistic techniques and principles resulted in his dismissal in 1785. Thereafter he worked on his own as a book illustrator and print maker, using the Japanese techniques of block printing. His illustrations of everyday life executed for the encyclopaedic Mangwa established his reputation as the leading exponent of ukiyo-e ('pictures of the passing world') whose charm is exceeded only by their technical accomplishment. Of his prolific series of colour prints, the best known are *Thirty-six Views of Mount Fuji* (1823–29) and *Hundred Views of Mount Fuji* (1834–35), but he also produced several shorter sets and individual works. His prints had a tremendous impact on the Western world. Quite by chance, some of his prints were used as packing material for some china sent to Felix Bracquemond in 1856, triggering off the enthusiasm for Japanese art which strongly influenced the Impressionists.

MOVEMENT

Ukiyo-e

OTHER WORKS

The Dream of the Fisherman's Wife

INFLUENCES

Hishikawa Moronobu, Ando Hiroshige

Katsushika Hokusai *Born* 1760 Edo (now Tokyo), Japan

Died 1849

Cole, Thomas

Mountain Sunrise, 1826

Courtesy of Private Collection/Christie's Images

Born in Lancashire, England, Thomas Cole served his apprenticeship as an engraver of textile designs for calico printing. He emigrated with his family in 1818 and worked briefly as an engraver in Philadelphia before settling in Steubenville, Ohio, where he took lessons from an unknown travelling artist. In 1823 he returned to Philadelphia and enrolled at the Pennsylvania Academy of Fine Arts, then moved to New York in 1825. He began sketching along the Hudson River and through the Catskill Mountains, and his paintings of the American wilderness brought him fame and fortune. In 1829–32 he travelled all over Europe painting landscapes and classical ruins. On his return to New York he embarked on a colossal project – a series of large paintings that would chronicle the rise and fall of civilization. He took immense pride in his allegories and deprecated the landscapes which made his fortune and on which his reputation still rests.

MOVEMENT

Hudson River School

OTHER WORKS

Expulsion from the Garden of Eden; The Course of Empire

INFLUENCES

Washington Alliston

Thomas Cole *Born* 1801, Lancashire, England

Died 1848

Delacroix, Eugène

Le Puits de la Casbah Tangier ('The Wells at the Tangier Kasbah')

Courtesy of Private Collection/Christie's Images

A champion of the Romantic cause, Delacroix was legally the son of a politician but in reality he was probably the illegitimate child of Talleyrand, a celebrated diplomat. He trained under Guérin, a respected Neoclassical painter, but the dominant influence on his style came from Géricault, a fellow pupil. Delacroix watched the latter creating *The Raft of the Medusa*, one of the seminal works of the Romantic movement, and was overwhelmed by its raw, emotional power. He swiftly began to emulate this in his own canvasses, achieving his breakthrough with *The Massacre of Chios*.

Critics attacked Delacroix for his apparent fixation with violence and his lack of finish. They accused him of wallowing in scenes of brutality, rather than acts of heroism. In addition, they denounced his pictures as 'sketches', because he abandoned the smooth, linear finish of the Neoclassical style, preferring to build up his compositions with small dabs of colour. Like most Romantics, Delacroix was fascinated with the exotic but, unusually, he actually visited the Arab world. As a result, his Orientalist paintings were more sober and realistic than most European fantasies.

MOVEMENT

Romanticism

OTHER WORKS

The Massacre at Chios; Women of Algiers; The Death of Sardanapalus

INFLUENCES

Rubens, Géricault, Constable

Eugène Delacroix *Born* 1798

Died 1863

Landseer, Sir Edwin

Saint Bernard Dogs

Courtesy of Private Collection, Christie's Images

Edwin Henry Landseer was taught by his father to sketch animals from life. From the age of 13 he exhibited at the Royal Academy and became one of the most fashionable painters of the mid-Victorian period, specializing in pictures of dogs with humanoid expressions and deer, usually set in misty, romantic Highland glens or moorland made popular by the novels of Sir Walter Scott and Queen Victoria's passion for Balmoral. Landseer's paintings attained even wider prominence as a result of the fine engravings of them produced by his brother Thomas. One of the Queen's favourite artists, he was knighted in 1850. He modelled the four lions, cast in bronze, which sit at the foot of Nelson's Column in Trafalgar Square, London, unveiled in 1867. Landseer's posthumous reputation was dented by accusations of sentimentalizing animals and, in more recent years, of political incorrectness in glorifying blood sports, but he wielded enormous influence on a later generation of British artists.

MOVEMENT

English School

OTHER WORKS

Monarch of the Glen; The Old Shepherd's Chief Mourner

INFLUENCES

George Stubbs

Sir Edwin Landseer *Born 1802 London*

Died 1873

Rousseau, Théodore

A Wooded Landscape at Sunset with a Faggot Gatherer

Courtesy of Christie's Images

A French landscape painter, Rousseau is hailed as the leader of the Barbizon School. The son of a clothier, Rousseau developed a deep love of the countryside at an early age. After working briefly in a sawmill, he decided to take up landscape painting and trained with Joseph Rémond. The latter produced classical landscapes, however, and Rousseau's naturalistic tendencies were better served by the study of foreign artists, such as Ruisdael and Constable. He adopted the practice of making sketches outdoor — a foretaste of Impressionism — although he still preferred to finish his paintings in the studio.

Rousseau's favourite location was the Barbizon region, at the edge of the Forest of Fontainebleau. By the late 1840s, this area had become the focus for a group of like-minded artists known as the Barbizon School. Headed by Rousseau, this circle included Corot, Daubigny, Diaz and Millet. In the 1850s, Rousseau's work achieved widespread recognition, fetching high prices, but he preferred to remain in Barbizon, campaigning to preserve the character of the forest. He died in his cottage, in the arms of fellow landscapist Jean-François Millet.

MOVEMENT

Barbizon School

OTHER WORKS

Edge of a Forest – Sunset; Farm in the Landes

INFLUENCES

Jacob van Ruisdael, Constable

Théodore Rousseau *Born* 1812 Paris, France

Died 1867

Turner, J. M. W.

The Burning of the Houses of Parliament (detail), c. 1834–35

On 16 October 1834 the Houses of Parliament went up in flames, an event that had a resounding impact on Turner, and when people flocked to the burning buildings in fascination, he was among them. It is not insignificant, as this was an area of London he had spent much of his childhood exploring, going up and down the Thames from his home in Covent Garden. The night of the fire Turner took his sketchbooks with him and finding a boat, sketched the scene from the river. His hasty sketches, done in pencil and in watercolour, were later used as a reference for two oil paintings of the scene.

The scene was the perfect subject matter for Turner, offering him the forum to paint those things that he loved the most, the effects of water, light, atmosphere and colour. The smoke and heat that he evokes in this watercolour is both acrid and hot to the viewer, and behind the haze he has captured the buildings precisely and finely through his careful use of line and form.

MOVEMENT

English School

SIMILAR WORKS

Naples or Land of Smouldering Fire Alfred William Hunt, 1871

MEDIUM

Watercolour and gouache on paper

Joseph Mallord William Turner *Born* 1775 London, England

Died 1851

Millais, Sir John Everett

Ferdinand Lured by Ariel, 1849

The subject is drawn from Act I, Scene II of *The Tempest*, where Ferdinand has been shipwrecked on Prospero's island. Ariel, the latter's servant, lures the young man towards his master by whispering the false news that his father has perished in the storm:

Full fathom five thy father lies; / Of his bones are corals made;

Those are pearls that were his eyes...

Ferdinand is baffled by the invisible informant ('Where should this music be? i' the air or the earth?'), but consents to be taken to Prospero, carried by the strange bats that are pictured on the left.

Millais' picture was a bold invention, quite unlike the stagey depictions of Shakespearean fairy subjects that were popular at the time. He took great care to make the human elements appear as realistic as possible. Ferdinand's outfit was taken from Camille Bonnard's *Costumes Historiques*, and the background details were painted with immense precision, right down to the lizard in the corner. In spite of this, he experienced some difficulty in selling the picture. A dealer had reserved it in advance, but withdrew his offer when he saw the finished work. He was disappointed, it appears, with the fairy elements, which lacked the coy eroticism that had become the norm in Victorian fairy scenes.

MOVEMENT

Pre-Raphaelite

SIMILAR WORKS

Puck (sculpture) by Thomas Woolner, 1845–47

MEDIUM

Oil on panel

Sir John Everett Millais *Born* 1829 Southampton, England

Died 1896

Paton, Sir Joseph Noël

The Quarrel of Oberon and Titania, 1849

This depicts the first encounter between Titania and Oberon in *A Midsummer Night's Dream*. He chides her for failing in her wifely duties by keeping the Indian boy from him. Titania accuses Oberon of stealing away from fairyland to play on his pipes and seduce young women, a detail that may have inspired Paton to include the statue of Pan on the right.

Paton had produced a smaller version of this scene in 1846, but this is his definitive treatment of the subject. It forms an obvious companion piece to *The Reconciliation of Oberon and Titania*. These two pictures did much to secure Paton's reputation. *The Reconciliation* won a £300 prize in the Westminster Hall Competition, while *The Quarrel* was received with great acclaim when it was exhibited at the Royal Scottish Academy in 1850. Critics were especially impressed by the amount of detail that he had managed to cram into the scene. Lewis Carroll (1832–98) reported excitedly that he counted 165 fairies when he saw the picture in 1857. Paton himself has often been described as the Scottish Pre-Raphaelite. He became a friend of John Millais (1829–96) when they trained together at the Royal Academy and, if he had not returned to Scotland in 1844, Paton would almost certainly have become a member of the Pre-Raphaelite Brotherhood.

MOVEMENT

Pre-Raphaelite

MEDIUM

Oil on canvas

SIMILAR WORKS

Isabella by Sir John Everett Millais, 1848–49

Sir Joseph Noël Paton *Born* 1821 Dunfermline, Scotland

Died 1901

Fitzgerald, John Anster

The Painter's Dream, 1857

This compelling work dates from the late 1850s, when Fitzgerald produced a series of paintings on the subject of sleep and dreams. Here the artist has fallen asleep in his chair. In his dream he sees himself painting a beautiful fairy. This same portrait is shown on the right, covered by a drape, where a mischievous spirit attempts to make his own amendments to it. There are suggestions that the sleep may be drug-induced. One of the creatures offers a large glass to the artist, while the female fairy sits under a purple convolvulus, which was known for its narcotic properties. The same flower was also featured prominently in *The Fairies' Banquet*. It is unclear whether these grotesque fairies were meant to be figments of the artist's imagination, appearing to him in his dream, or whether they were meant to be genuinely threatening him in his studio. Either way the picture makes an interesting comparison with a similar painting that Charles Doyle (1832–93), father of Richard Doyle, produced during his confinement in the Montrose asylum. *In Self-Portrait, A Meditation* Doyle pictured depicted himself in the company of a group of equally menacing figures. The difference was, however, that Doyle was wide awake and the demons seemed all too real.

MOVEMENT

Romanticism

SIMILAR WORKS

Self-Portrait, A Meditation by Charles Altamont Doyle, c. 1885–93

MEDIUM

Oil on millboard

John Anster Fitzgerald *Born* 1832 London, England

Died 1906

The Age of Impressionism

1850–1900

Courbet, Gustave

Bonjour Monsieur Courbet, 1854

Courtesy of Musée Fabre, Montpelier, France/Bridgeman Art Library

A French painter, Courbet was the leader of the Realist movement. Born at Ornans in the Jura region, Courbet remained fiercely loyal to this area throughout his life, featuring it prominently in his paintings. Although he later claimed to be self-taught, he actually studied under a succession of minor artists, but learned more from copying old masters in the Louvre. Initially, Courbet aimed for conventional success by exhibiting at the Salon, even winning a gold medal for his 1849 entry. After he showed *The Burial at Ornans*, however, official approval evaporated. Instead, this landmark realist picture was savagely criticized for being too large, too ugly and too meaningless. Worse still, in the light of the recent 1848 Revolution, the artist was suspected of having a political agenda.

Courbet revelled in the furore. In the following years, he gained greater recognition abroad, but remained antagonistic towards the French Establishment. He refused to exhibit at the 1855 World Fair, turned down the offer of a Legion of Honour and served as a Councillor in the Paris Commune. The latter proved his undoing and he was forced to spend his final years exiled in Switzerland.

MOVEMENT

Realism

OTHER WORKS

The Painter's Studio; The Bathers

INFLUENCES

The Le Nain brothers, Velázquez, Millet

Gustave Courbet *Born* 1819 France

Died 1877

Corot, Jean-Baptiste-Camille
Etretat un Moulin à Vent, 1855

Courtesy of Private Collection/Christie's Images

Corot, a French painter, specialized in landscapes in the classical tradition. Born in Paris, Corot was the son of a cloth merchant and initially followed his father's trade. For a time, he worked at The Caliph of Bagdad, a luxury fabric shop. Turning to art, he trained under Michallon and Bertin, both of whom were renowned for their classical landscapes. Indeed, Michallon was the first winner of the Historical Landscape category in the Prix de Rome, when it was introduced in 1817. This genre, which Corot was to make his own, consisted of idealized views, set in the ancient, classical world, and was inspired by the 17th century paintings of Poussin and Claude Lorrain.

Corot's distinctive style stemmed from his unique blend of modern and traditional techniques. Each summer, he made lengthy sketching trips around Europe, working these studies up into paintings in the winter, in his Paris studio. He combined this traditional practice with a fascination for the latest developments in photography. The shimmering appearance of his foliage, for example, was inspired by the *halation* or blurring effects, which could be found in contemporary photographs.

MOVEMENT

Romanticism, Barbizon School

OTHER WORKS

The Bridge at Narni; Gust of Wind; Recollection of Mortefontaine

INFLUENCES

Achille-Etna Michallon, Claude Lorrain, Constable

Jean-Baptiste-Camille Corot *Born* 1796

Died 1875

Millet, Jean-François
La Cardeuse, c. 1858

Courtesy of Private Collection/Christie's Images

Millet was born near the city of Cherbourg, which granted him a scholarship to train in Paris, under Delaroche. His early paintings were mainly portraits or pastoral idylls, but by the 1840s he was producing more naturalistic scenes of the countryside. These drew on his own experience, since he came from peasant stock, but the pictures disturbed some critics, because of their unglamorous view of rustic life.

In the 1850s Millet's work attracted genuine hostility. In part, this was due to fears that his paintings were political. Memories of the 1848 Revolution were still very fresh, and the authorities were nervous about any images with socialist overtones. Millet declined to express his political views, but *The Gleaners*, for example, was a compelling portrait of rural poverty. Some critics also linked his work with the Realist movement, launched by Courbet, which was widely seen as an attack on the academic establishment.

After 1849, Millet was mainly based at Barbizon, where he befriended Rousseau and other members of the Barbizon School. Under their influence, he devoted the latter part of his career to landscape painting.

MOVEMENTS

Naturalism, Barbizon School

OTHER WORKS

The Winnower; Man with a Hoe

INFLUENCES

Rousseau, the Le Nain brothers, Gustave Courbert

Jean-François Millet *Born* 1814 France

Died 1875

Palmer, Samuel

Illustrations to *Milton's Lycidas, c. 1864*

Courtesy of Private Collection/Christie's Images

Born in London, the son of an eccentric bookseller, Palmer revealed his artistic talent at a very early stage. In 1819, aged just 14, he exhibited at the Royal Academy and the British Institution, selling a painting at the latter. Three years later he met the painter John Linnell, who gave him some instruction. More importantly, perhaps, Linnell also introduced Palmer to William Blake – a meeting which only served to intensify the youngster's mystical outlook.

In 1824, the same year as his encounter with Blake, Palmer started painting at Shoreham in Kent. In this rural retreat, he began to produce the strange, pastoral idylls, which made his name. Using nothing more than ink and a sepia wash, he conjured up a worldly paradise, stocked with dozing shepherds, carefree animals and luxuriant foliage. In 1826, Palmer settled in Shoreham, where he was soon joined by a group of like-minded artists, who came to be known as the Ancients. Sadly, Palmer's period of poetic inspiration was short-lived. By the mid-1830s, his paintings had become disappointingly conventional, although his etchings retained some of his earlier, lyrical power.

MOVEMENTS

Romanticism, the Ancients

OTHER WORKS

The Sleeping Shepherd; Coming from Evening Church

INFLUENCES

William Blake, John Linnell, Edward Calvert

Samuel Palmer *Born* 1805 London, England

Died 1881

Rossetti, Dante Gabriel

Reverie, 1868

Courtesy of Christie's Images

Rossetti came from a hugely talented family. His father was a noted scholar while his sister Christina became a celebrated poet. For years Dante wavered between a career in art or literature, before devoting himself to painting. While still only 20, he helped to found the Pre-Raphaelite Brotherhood, the radical group that shook the Victorian art world with their controversial exhibits at the Royal Academy in 1848. The Pre-Raphaelites were appalled by the dominant influence of sterile, academic art, which they linked with the teachings of Raphael – then regarded as the greatest Western painter. In its place, they called for a return to the purity and simplicity of medieval and early Renaissance art.

Although championed by the critic Ruskin the Pre-Raphaelites' efforts were greeted with derision and this discouraged Rossetti from exhibiting again. During the 1850s, he concentrated largely on watercolours, but in the following decade he began producing sensuous oils of women. These were given exotic and mysterious titles, such as *Monna Vanna* and were effectively the precursors of the *femmes fatales*, which were so admired by the Symbolists.

MOVEMENT

Pre-Raphaelite Brotherhood

OTHER WORKS

Beata Beatrix; Proserpine

INFLUENCES

Ford Madox Brown, William Bell Scott

Dante Gabriel Rossetti *Born* 1828

Died 1882

Burne-Jones, Edward Coley

The Briar Rose Series 4: *The Sleeping Beauty*, 1870–90

© Faringdon Collection, Buscot, Oxon, UK/www.bridgeman.co.uk

Edward Coley Burne-Jones was a contemporary of William Morris and Dante Gabriel Rossetti and was greatly influenced by both men. Burne-Jones left Oxford University without graduating, having sensed that his future career lay not in the church, for which he had been preparing, but in the arts. After travelling in France and Italy Burne-Jones applied himself to painting, a medium in which he was largely self-taught. His work, influenced by Rossetti, Michelangelo and Botticelli, combined mystical and mythical figures with Romanticism. Like other Pre-Raphaelite artists, Burne-Jones found inspiration in medieval stories of chivalry, romance and ethereal heroes and heroines. Many of his paintings are subtle in their eroticism and inspired later Symbolists. His delicately sensuous lines inspired the work of Aubrey Beardsley (1872–98).

Burne-Jones collaborated with William Morris when they, with others, established Morris, Marshall, Faulkner and Co. in 1861 to promote the Arts and Crafts movement. The members of the fraternity experimented with different media and Burne-Jones designed stained-glass windows for the Church.

MOVEMENT

Pre-Raphaelite

SIMILAR WORKS

Flight Into Egypt, stained-glass window designed for St Michael's Church, Brighton by Edward Burne-Jones

MEDIUM

Oil on canvas

Edward Coley Burne-Jones *Born* 1833 Birmingham, England

Died 1898

Doré, Gustave

A Midsummer Night's Dream, c. 1870

© Sotheby's Picture Library

Doré's balletic picture serves as a reminder that for much of its history *A Midsummer Night's Dream* was performed as a spectacle of music and dance, rather than a traditional play. Generations of directors found it virtually impossible to stage and made savage cuts to the text. It was performed only once during the Restoration period, when Pepys praised the dancing but condemned the rest as "the most insipid ridiculous play that I ever saw in my life". In his version, David Garrick (1717–79) removed all but 600 lines of the original text, basing the performance around the antics of the fairies and the lovers.

A greater sense of balance was restored by Madame Lucia Vestris. In her 1840 production she restored most of Shakespeare's text, although opera and ballet still took precedence over drama. In particular, during the supernatural scenes, the stage was filled with crowds of female fairies wearing costumes made of white gauze. This became a feature of many productions throughout the nineteenth century and clearly provided the inspiration for Doré's picture. In her production Vestris actually took the part of Oberon herself. This started a trend for both the fairy rulers to be played by women. Traditionally Oberon was a contralto, while Titania was a soprano.

MOVEMENT

Romanticism

SIMILAR WORKS

A Midsummer Night's Dream by Thomas Grieve, 1856

MEDIUM

Oil on canvas

Gustave Doré   *Born* 1832 Strasbourg, France

Died 1883

Whistler, James

Nocturne: Blue and Silver – Chelsea, 1871

This was the first in the series of Nocturne paintings that Whistler executed, and depicts the view from Battersea Bridge across the Thames to Chelsea, with the tower of Chelsea Old Church barely visible on the right hand side. According to correspondence written by the artist's mother, this was the second painting that Whistler had done on the same day, having earlier painted *Variations in Violet and Green*. This daylight portrayal of a similar view as the Nocturne shows the influence that Japanese and Oriental art was having on Whistler's work. The Nocturne picture of Chelsea was painted on a wooden panel, his colours being applied over a dark grey primer that helps to achieve the glowing luminosity and translucent beauty of the scene. The artist Edward J. Poynter (1836-1919) wrote to Whistler after seeing both views of Chelsea in 1871, saying, 'perhaps you will allow me to say how very much I admire both the paintings, but especially the moonlight, which renders the poetical side of the scene better than any moonlight picture I ever saw.' This was high praise indeed. Poynter was one of the great Victorian Classical painters and was firmly established within the British art establishment – a privilege that Whistler never enjoyed. Poynter went on to be elected President of the RA in 1896, and was Director of the National Gallery from 1894 to 1904.

MOVEMENT

Impressionism

SIMILAR WORKS

Whitby Fishing Boats John Singer Sargent, 1885

MEDIUM

Oil on wood

James Abbott McNeill Whistler *Born* 1834 Lowell, Massachusetts, USA

Died 1903

Morisot, Berthe

Enfant dans les Roses Trémières

One of the leading female Impressionists. The daughter of a high-ranking civil servant, Morisot received art lessons from Corot. Then in 1859, she met Fantin-Latour, who would later introduce her to future members of the Impressionist circle. Before this, she had already made her mark at the Salon, winning favourable reviews for two landscapes shown at the 1864 exhibition. Conventional success beckoned, but a meeting with Manet in 1868 altered the course of Morisot's career. She was strongly influenced by his radical style, and appeared as a model in several of his paintings. For her part, she also had an impact on Manet's art, by persuading him to experiment with *plein-air* painting. The close links between the two artists were further reinforced when Morisot married Manet's brother in 1874.

Morisot proved to be one of the most committed members of the Impressionist group, exhibiting in all but one of their shows. She concentrated principally on quiet, domestic scenes, typified by *The Cradle*, which depicts her sister Edma with her newborn child. These canvasses displayed Morisot's gift for spontaneous brushwork and her feeling for the different nuances of light.

MOVEMENT

Impressionism

OTHER WORKS

Summer's Day; The Lake in the Bois de Boulogne

INFLUENCES

Manet, Renoir, Corot

Berthe Morisot *Born 1841*

Died 1895

Rousseau, Henri

Vue de l'Isle Saint-Louis, Prise du Port Saint-Nicolas le Soir

Courtesy of Private Collection/Christie's Images

A French painter, perhaps the most famous of all Naïve artists, Rousseau came from a poor background and went through a succession of menial jobs before turning to art late in life. Among other things he was a clerk, a soldier and a toll-collector. While working as the latter, he began painting as a hobby and, in 1893, he took early retirement, in order to pursue his artistic ambitions. Rousseau was entirely self-taught, although he did take advice from academic artists such as Clément and Gérôme. He copied many of the individual elements in his pictures from book illustrations, using a mechanical device called a pantograph. But it was his dreamlike combination of images and his intuitive sense of colour which gave his art its unique appeal. Rousseau began exhibiting his paintings from the mid-1880s, using avant-garde bodies such as the Salon des Indépendants, for the simple reason that they had no selection committee. He never achieved great success, but his guileless personality won him many friends in the art world, among them Picasso, Apollinaire and Delaunay. Posthumously, his work was an important influence on the Surrealists.

MOVEMENT

Naïve Art

OTHER WORKS

Surprised! (Tropical Storm with a Tiger); The Sleeping Gypsy

INFLUENCES

Jean-Léon Gérôme, Félix Clément

Henri Rousseau *Born 1844 France*

Died 1910

Grimshaw, John Atkinson

Iris, 1876

© Sotheby's Picture Library

Grimshaw produced several variations of this theme. Most depict Iris, a messenger of the gods, who was turned into a rainbow after failing to wither the summer plants at the start of autumn. The painting is notable for the unusual pose of the figure as well as the eerie lighting. Iris's arms are folded across her chest and her eyes are closed as though she is asleep or dead. Prior to the nineteenth century artists had occasionally portrayed Iris in the kingdom of sleep. This occurred when Hera sent the goddess to rouse Morpheus, the god of dreams. In some variants of this picture, Grimshaw identified the figure as the spirit of the night. Here the link is that, according to Greek mythology, Sleep (Hypnos) was the son of Night (Nyx). The mysterious glow around the figure has led to suggestions that Grimshaw was influenced by the contemporary vogue for spiritualism and that the shimmering creature might actually be interpreted as a form of ectoplasm. The artist may have drawn some inspiration from this trend as the debate about spiritualism was certainly topical, but there is no evidence that he had any personal interest in the subject.

MOVEMENT

Romanticism

SIMILAR WORKS

Twilight Fantasies by Edward Robert Hughes, 1911

MEDIUM

Oil on canvas

John Atkinson Grimshaw *Born* 1836 Leeds, England

Died 1893

Degas, Edgar

Danseuses Vertes, 1878

Courtesy of Private Collection/Christie's Images

A French painter and graphic artist, Degas was one of the leading members of the Impressionist circle. Originally destined for the law, Degas's early artistic inspiration came from the Neoclassical painter Ingres – who taught him the value of sound draughtsmanship – and from his study of the old masters. However, he changed direction dramatically after a chance meeting with Manet in 1861. Manet introduced him to the Impressionist circle and, in spite of his somewhat aloof manner, Degas was welcomed into the group, participating in most of their shows.

Degas was not a typical Impressionist, having little enthusiasm for either landscape or *plein-air* painting but he was, nevertheless, extremely interested in capturing the spontaneity of a momentary image. Where most artists sought to present a well-constructed composition, Degas wanted his pictures to look like an uncomposed snapshot; he often showed figures from behind or bisected by the picture frame. Similarly, when using models, he tried to avoid aesthetic, classical poses, preferring to show them yawning, stretching or carrying out mundane tasks. These techniques are seen to best effect in Degas' two favourite subjects: scenes from the ballet and horse-racing.

MOVEMENT

Impressionism

OTHER WORKS

The Dancing Class; Carriage at the Races; Absinthe

INFLUENCES

Jean-Auguste-Dominique Ingres, Edouard Manet

Edgar Degas *Born* 1834 France

Died 1917

Manet, Edouard

La Rue Mosnier aux Drapeaux, 1878

An influential French painter, Manet was regarded by many as the inspirational force behind the Impressionist movement. Coming from a wealthy family, Manet trained under the history painter Couture, but was chiefly influenced by his study of the Old Masters, particularly Velázquez. His aim was to achieve conventional success through the Salon, but ironically two controversial pictures cast him in the role of artistic rebel. *Le Déjeuner sur l'Herbe* and *Olympia* were both updated versions of Renaissance masterpieces, but the combination of classical nudes and a modern context scandalized Parisian critics. This very modernity, however, appealed strongly to a group of younger artists, who were determined to paint scenes of modern life, rather than subjects from the past. This circle of friends who gathered around Manet at the Café Guerbois were to become the Impressionists.

Manet was equivocal about the new movement. He enjoyed the attention of his protégés, but still hoped for official success and, as a result, did not participate in the Impressionist exhibitions. Even so, he was eventually persuaded to try open-air painting, and his later pictures display a lighter palette and a freer touch.

MOVEMENTS

Realism, Impressionism

OTHER WORKS

A Bar at the Folies-Bergère

INFLUENCES

Velázquez, Gustave Courbet

Edouard Manet *Born* 1832 France

Died 1883

Renoir, Pierre-Auguste

Les Baigneuses

Courtesy of Private Collection/Christie's Images

A French Impressionist, born in Limoges, Renoir trained as a porcelain-painter before entering the studio of Gleyre in 1862. He learnt little from this master, but did meet future members of the Impressionist circle who were fellow-pupils. Together they attended the meetings at the Café Guerbois, where Manet held court. Initially, Renoir was particularly close to Monet and the pair often painted side by side on the River Seine. Although both were desperately poor, these early, apparently carefree pictures are often cited as the purest distillation of Impressionist principles.

Renoir participated at four of the Impressionist shows, but gradually distanced himself from the movement. This was partly because of his growing success as a portraitist, and partly because he had never lost his affection for Old Masters such as Rubens and Boucher. In the early 1880s, he reached a watershed in his career. He married Aline Charigot, one of his models, and travelled widely in Europe and North Africa, reaffirming his taste for the art of the past. In his subsequent work, he moved away from traditional Impressionist themes, concentrating instead on sumptuous nudes.

MOVEMENT

Impressionism

OTHER WORKS

The Luncheon of the Boating Party; The Bathers; The Umbrellas,

INFLUENCES

Monet, François Boucher, Rubens

Pierre-Auguste Renoir *Born* 1841 *France*

Died 1919

Sisley, Alfred

Le Barrage de Saint Mammes, 1885

Courtesy of Private Collection/Christie's Images

Born in Paris of English parents, Alfred Sisley had a conventional art education in Paris and at first was strongly influenced by Corot. In 1862 he entered the studio of Charles Gleyre, where he was a fellow pupil with Monet and Renoir, whom he joined on sketching and painting expeditions to Fontainebleau. The range of colours employed by Sisley lightened significantly under the influence of his companions. From 1874 onwards he exhibited regularly with the Impressionists and is regarded as the painter who remained most steadfast to the aims and ideals of that movement. The vast majority of his works are landscapes, drawing on the valleys of the Loire, Seine and Thames for most of his subjects. Sisley revelled in the subtleties of cloud formations and the effects of light, especially in the darting reflection of water. Hopeless at the business aspects of his art and largely dependent on his father for money, Sisley spent his last years in great poverty. Like Van Gogh, interest in his paintings only developed after his death.

MOVEMENT

Impressionism

OTHER WORKS

Wooden Bridge at Argenteuil; Snow at Veneux-Nadon

INFLUENCES

Corot, Paul Renoir, Monet, Charles Gleyre

Alfred Sisley *Born* 1839 Paris, France

Died 1899

Alma-Tadema, Sir Lawrence

Roses of Heliogabalus, 1888

Courtesy of Private Collection/Christie's Images

Lawrence Alma-Tadema trained at the Antwerp Academy of Art and later studied under Baron Hendryk Leys, an artist noted for his large historical paintings. In 1863 Alma-Tadema went to Italy, whose classical remains, notably at Pompeii, exerted a great influence on him. He moved to England in 1870, where he built up a reputation for narrative paintings in the Classical style. He was knighted in 1899. Three years later he visited Egypt and the impact of Pharaonic civilization had a major impact on the works of his last years. His large paintings brought everyday scenes of long-dead civilizations vividly to life through his extraordinary mastery of detail. He amassed a vast collection of ancient artefacts, photographs and sketches from his travels; the visual aids that enabled him to recreate the ancient world.

MOVEMENT

Neoclassical

OTHER WORKS

The Finding of Moses; The Conversion of Paula

INFLUENCES

Baron Hendryk Leys

Sir Lawrence Alma-Tadema *Born* 1836 Dronrijp, Holland

Died 1912

Seurat, Georges

Les Poseuses, 1887–88

Courtesy of Private Collection/Christie's Images

Georges Pierre Seurat studied at the École des Beaux-Arts and was influenced by the precise draughtsmanship of Ingres, as well as with Chevreul's theories on colour. He combined the Classicist tradition with the newer ideas of the Impressionists. In particular, he painted in a very distinctive style using a multitude of different coloured dots to build up the impression of the subject, much as the half-tone process or multicolour photogravure use a screen of dots of varying intensity and depth to achieve the overall image. This extremely precise method he termed divisionism, and it was instrumental in the subsequent development of pointillism. There is not much evidence of this technique, however, in his first major work depicting bathers at Asnières (1884), but it became almost a trade mark in his later paintings. Always meticulous in the execution of his work, Seurat was also painstaking in the preparation, often spending months on preliminary sketches for each canvas.

MOVEMENT

French Impressionism

OTHER WORKS

The Can-Can; Sunday Afternoon on the Island of the Grande Jatte

INFLUENCES

Ingres, Eugène Chevreul

Georges Seurat *Born* 1859 Paris, France

Died 1891

Pissarro, Camille

Jeune Paysanne à sa Toilette, 1888

Courtesy of Private Collection/Christie's Images

A French painter, Pisarro was one of the founding fathers of Impressionism. Born at St Thomas in the West Indies, Pissarro was schooled in Paris and enjoyed a brief interlude in Venezuela, before eventually settling in France in 1855. There, he was initially influenced by Corot, whose landscapes he admired at the Universal Exhibition. He also studied at the Académie Suisse, where he met Monet, who introduced him to the future Impressionist circle at the Café Guerbois. Pissarro remained in close contact with Monet in 1870–71, when both men took refuge in London during the Franco-Prussian War.

Pissarro was slightly older than the other Impressionists and this, together with his ability as a teacher, enabled him to assume a guru-like authority within the group. In the mid-1880s, Pissarro flirted briefly with Seurat's Neo-Impressionist techniques, before reverting to his traditional style. In later years, he had increasing trouble with his eyesight and could no longer paint out of doors. Instead, he took to painting lively street scenes from rented hotel rooms. His son Lucien also became a successful artist.

MOVEMENT

Impressionism

OTHER WORKS

View of Pontoise; A Road in Louveciennes; Red Roofs

INFLUENCES

Corot, Monet, Seurat

Camille Pissarro *Born* 1830

Died 1903

Sargent, John Singer
Women at Work

Born of American parents in Florence, Italy, John Singer Sargent was brought up in Nice, Rome and Dresden – giving him a rather sporadic education but a very cosmopolitan outlook. He studied painting and drawing in each of these cities, but his only formal schooling came at the Accademia in Florence, where he won a prize in 1873, and in the studio of Carolus-Duran in Paris (1874). In 1876 he paid the first of many trips to the USA, re-affirming his American citizenship in that Centennial year. He painted landscapes, but it was his early portraits that earned him acclaim. However, the scurrilous treatment of him by the French press over a décolleté portrait of Madame Gautreau induced him to leave France in 1885 and settle in London, where he spent most of his life. As well as portraits he produced large decorative works for public buildings from 1910 onwards. Some of his most evocative paintings were produced as a war artist in 1914–18.

MOVEMENT

Anglo-American School

OTHER WORKS

The Lady of the Rose; Carmencita; Gassed

INFLUENCES

Carolus-Duran, Frans Hals, Velázquez

John Singer Sargent *Born* 1856 Florence, Italy

Died 1925

Monet, Claude

Haystacks, Hazy Sunshine, 1891

Monet's Haystack series was apparently begun somewhat by chance. Monet would often recount how one day he was painting a haystack in a field behind his house and the light kept changing, altering the colours and tonality that he could use. He asked Blanche Hoschedé, who was assisting him at the time, to keep bringing him a new canvas and that is how the monumental series first took off.

During the winter months the sunlight had a peculiar quality and radiance, quite different from that during the summer, and Monet embarked on a series of winter effects. The reflection from the white of the snow and frost afforded him a whole new set of light nuances to capture.

In this painting, *Haystacks, Hazy Sunshine*, the topographical realism of the haystack within the landscape is all but gone. There is nothing but the haystack itself and the colour of the light. He has used a heavy cross hatching of short brushstrokes of soft pinks, whites, blues and yellows to build up the overall luminosity of the canvas. The single haystack stands alone surrounded by ethereal light, which lends it an air of magical unearthliness.

MOVEMENT

Impressionism

SIMILAR WORKS

Landscape at Eragny Camille Pissarro, 1895

MEDIUM

Oil on canvas

Claude Monet *Born* 1840 Paris, France

Died 1926

von Menzel, Adolph

Auf der Fahrt durch Schone Natur, 1892

Courtesy of Private Collection/Christie's Images

The son of a schoolmaster and lithographer, Adolph von Menzel was taught by his father and made his debut at an exhibition in Breslau in 1828 with a drawing of a tigress. The family moved to Berlin in 1830, where Adolph was employed in his father's business as a draughtsman and book illustrator. At the Berlin Academy show (1833) he exhibited illustrations for the works of Goethe. Later he produced a series showing the uniforms of the Prussian army and woodcut engravings of historical subjects. Inspired by the French Revolution of 1848 he painted his first great historic work, *The Lying in State of the March Fallen* – the first German political painting. Later he produced numerous portraits and historical scenes and was employed as a war artist during the Seven Weeks' War (1866) and the Franco-German War (1870–71), for which he was awarded the Ordre Pour le Mérite, Prussia's highest decoration. A pillar of the establishment, he influenced the heroic style of German painting in the late nineteenth century.

MOVEMENT

German Romanticism

OTHER WORKS

Chess Players; Coronation of Wilhelm I in Königsberg

INFLUENCES

Claude Monet

Adolph von Menzel *Born* 1815 Breslau, Germany (now Wroclaw, Poland)

Died 1905

Liebermann, Max

Bathers on the Beach at Scheveningen, c. 1897–98

After his early training in Weimar, Germany, Max Liebermann continued his studies in Amsterdam and Paris, one of the first German artists of his generation to go abroad and come under the influence of foreign painters – in his case Courbet, Millet and the Barbizon School. Returning to Germany in 1878 Liebermann quickly established himself as the leading Impressionist, noted for his canvasses of mundane subjects in which elderly people and peasants predominate, although he also produced some noteworthy paintings of more sophisticated subjects, especially the outdoor cafés.

Liebermann played a major role in the establishment of the Berlin Secession in 1899. A major innovator in his heyday, he failed to move with the times and was later eclipsed by the younger avant-garde artists, led by Emil Nolde. Nevertheless, he remained a highly influential figure in German art, where the fashion for the heroic and romantic assured his works a substantial following.

MOVEMENT

German Impressionism

OTHER WORKS

The Parrot Keeper; Haarlem Pig Market

INFLUENCES

Courbet, Millet

Max Liebermann *Born* 1847 Berlin, Germany

Died 1935

Lavery, Sir John

The French Consulate, The Grand Canal, Venice

Courtesy of Private Collection/Christie's Images/By Courtesy of Felix Rosentiel's Widow & Son Ltd, London on behalf of the Estate of Sir John Lavery

Orphaned at the age of three, John Lavery, born in Belfast, was raised by relatives in Scotland and began his artistic career retouching photographs. When his studio burned down he used the insurance money to acquire an artistic education in London and Paris. Returning to Glasgow in 1885 he founded the group known as the Glasgow School, which promoted the techniques of French Impressionism in Britain. He excelled in landscapes and genre subjects but it was his skill as a portraitist that earned him his biggest commission, to paint the visit of Queen Victoria in 1888, a task that involved over 250 sitters and took two years to complete. The most cosmopolitan British artist of his generation, he spent much of his time in Brittany. He was knighted in 1918 but later devoted much of his energies to promoting better relations between Ireland and Britain. His portrait of his wife Hazel adorned Irish banknotes for many years.

MOVEMENT

Modern British School

OTHER WORKS

The Unfinished Harmony; George Bernard Shaw

INFLUENCES

Pre-Raphaelites, French Impressionists

Sir John Lavery *Born* 1856 Belfast, Ireland

Died 1941

Cassatt, Mary

The Young Mother, 1900

Courtesy of Private Collection/Christie's Images

Mary Cassatt studied art at the Pennsylvania Academy of Art in Philadelphia from 1861 to 1865, but after the American Civil War she travelled to Europe, continuing her studies in Spain, Italy and the Netherlands before settling in Paris, where she became a pupil of Edgar Degas. Her main work consisted of lithographs, etchings and drypoint studies of genre and domestic subjects which often reflect her interest in Japanese prints; but her reputation now rests on her larger works, executed in pastels or oils, which explore the tender relationship between mother and child, although her mastery of technique (which owed much to her original teacher, Thomas Eakins) prevented her from descending into the banal or mawkish. After her death in Paris in 1926 her work was neglected for some time, but in more recent years it has been the subject of re-appraisal and her realistic but sensitive portraiture of women, girls and young children is now more fully appreciated.

MOVEMENT

Impressionism

OTHER WORKS

Mother and Child; Woman Sewing

INFLUENCES

Thomas Eakins, Degas

Mary Cassatt *Born 1844 Pennsylvania, USA*

Died 1926

Hunt, William Holman

Master Hilary – The Tracer, 1900

Courtesy of Private Collection/Christie's Images

Hunt was an English painter and one of the founders of the Pre-Raphaelite movement. Born in London, the son of a warehouse manager, Hunt worked as a clerk before entering the Royal Academy School in 1844. There, he met Millais and, together with Rossetti, they formed the core of the Pre-Raphaelite Brotherhood. Hunt's meticulous attention to detail and his fondness for symbolism accorded well with the aims of the group, but his deeply felt religious convictions led him away from the British art scene. In January 1854, he embarked on a two-year expedition to Egypt and the Holy Land, believing that this was the only way to produce realistic images of biblical themes.

The critical response to this enterprise was mixed. *The Scapegoat* was greeted with puzzlement, but *The Finding of the Saviour in the Temple* was received far more enthusiastically, securing Hunt's reputation as a religious painter. Further trips to the East followed, although these were not always happy affairs. In 1866, his wife died in Florence, shortly after giving birth to their son. Hunt later married her sister. In 1905, he wrote his memoirs, which have become a primary source document for the Pre-Raphaelite movement.

MOVEMENT

Pre-Raphaelite Brotherhood

OTHER WORKS

The Hireling Shepherd; The Light of the World

INFLUENCES

Dante Gabriel Rossetti, Augustus Egg, John Everett Millais

William Holman Hunt *Born* 1827

Died 1910

The Age of Post-Impressionism

1880–1915

Stanhope, John Roddam Spencer
Love and the Maiden, 1877

Throughout his career, Stanhope was closely associated with the Pre-Raphaelite circle. He helped paint the murals in the Oxford Union, he had a studio next to Rossetti and he was a lifelong friend of Burne-Jones. He also shared their interests, most notably their devotion to early Italian art. This picture, for example, has affinities with Botticelli's (*c.* 1445–1510) *Primavera*. The dancers in the background are reminiscent of the Graces, while the profusion of flowers helps to conjure up a dreamlike atmosphere.

Stylistically Stanhope was chiefly influenced by Burne-Jones. His figures have the same pale, languid air. He also followed the latter's experiments with 'subjectless' paintings, paintings that evoked a mood rather than a specific storyline. In this instance, Stanhope appears to be depicting a scene from a Classical legend or a literary source, but neither of these is clearly identified. The title is deliberately vague. Instead the artist offers his public the suggestion of a romance: a young woman has apparently been struck by one of Cupid's arrows and gazes up adoringly at the love god, while he hurries off, seemingly oblivious to her. From these bare elements the spectator must use their imagination to create their own narrative.

MOVEMENT

Pre-Raphaelite/Art Nouveau

SIMILAR WORKS

The Bower Meadow by Dante Gabriel Rossetti, 1872

Love Among the Ruins by Sir Edward Coley Burne-Jones, 1870–73

MEDIUM

Tempera with gold paint and gold leaf on canvas

John Roddam Spencer Stanhope *Born* 1829 Barnsley, England

Died 1908

van Gogh, Vincent
Portrait de l'Artiste sans Barbe, 1889

Courtesy of Private Collection/Christie's Images

A leading Post-Impressionist and forerunner of Expressionism, van Gogh's first job was for a firm of art dealers, but he was sacked after a failed affair affected his ability to work. After a brief stint as a teacher, he became a lay preacher in a Belgian mining district. Here again he was fired when the Church became concerned at his over-zealous attempts to help the poor. Van Gogh had at least found his true vocation: illustrating the plight of the local peasantry.

Previously influenced by Millet, in 1886 van Gogh went to Paris where his style changed dramatically. Under the combined impact of Impressionism and Japanese prints, his palette lightened and he began to employ bold simplifications of form. Like Gauguin, he also used colours symbolically, rather than naturalistically. With financial help from his brother, Theo, van Gogh moved to the south of France. Gauguin joined him but the pair soon clashed, hastening van Gogh's mental collapse. Despite his illness he continued working at a frenzied pace until his suicide in July 1890. Van Gogh sold only one painting in his lifetime, but his work has since become the most popular and sought-after of any modern artist.

MOVEMENT

Post-Impressionism

OTHER WORKS

A Starry Night; Sunflowers; The Potato Eaters

INFLUENCES

Jean-François Millet, Louis Anquetin, Gauguin

Vincent van Gogh *Born* 1853

Died 1890

de Toulouse-Lautrec, Henri

Ambassadeurs: Aristide Bruant, 1892

The subject of this lithograph was Aristide Bruant (1851–1925) a singer and entertainer who embodied the spirit of the Montmartre nightlife that Toulouse-Lautrec found so inspiring. Bruant published illustrated papers to which the French artist contributed and also commissioned Toulouse-Lautrec to design posters, such as this one, to promote his cabaret act. The posters decorated the walls of the cabaret and were placed around Paris, bringing the artist to the attention of many ordinary people in the city. Bruant was a captivating and imposing man, who wore a trademark wide-brimmed hat and red scarf, perfectly captured in this print. This powerful, strident image is dramatic in its composition and the restrained use of colour.

The two men were friends for a number of years and Bruant introduced Toulouse-Lautrec to many of the entertainers whom he painted and sketched. The artist became a familiar sight at clubs and bars as he intently observed then sketched the men and women who populated them. He drank heavily in the evenings while sketching and during the day he revised and improved his drawings in the studio.

MOVEMENT

Art Nouveau

OTHER WORKS

Poster for Aristide Bruant in his cabaret

MEDIUM

Colour lithograph

Henri de Toulouse-Lautrec *Born* 1864 Albi, France

Died 1901

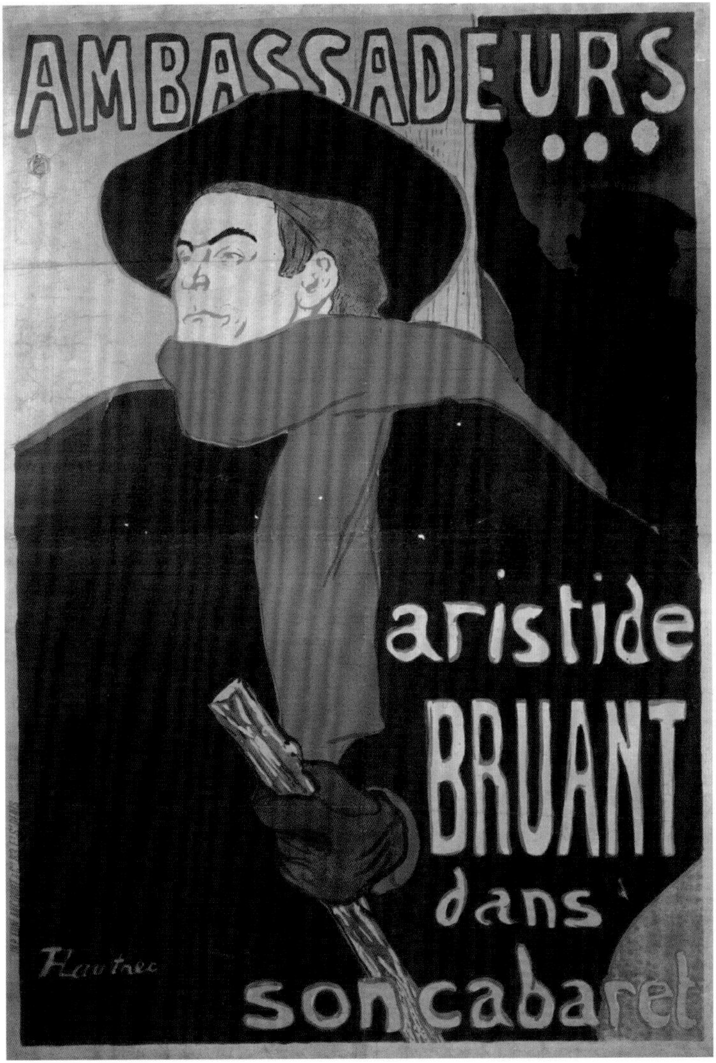
AMBASSADEURS
aristide
BRUANT
dans
son cabaret
HLautrec

Livemont, Privat

The Scent of a Rose, c. 1890

Courtesy of Christie's Images Ltd, 2005/© DACS 2005

Posters of the *belle époque* came to symbolize the popular culture of the countries where they were produced. In Paris a prevailing café culture was revealed in posters advertising alcoholic drinks, such as Privat Livemont's poster for Robette Absinthe, and the posters of Toulouse-Lautrec portray the decadence of Parisian nightlife in all its splendour. Spanish posters invited the public to come and witness the traditional bullfights; in the United Kingdom and United States, literary works and circuses were advertised. Each nation adopted the poster as a medium through which stories of mundane things and extraordinary events of everyday life could be told. Feminine, romantic and stylized women amidst fussy backdrops often featured in Livemont's advertising posters: this particular image was used to sell perfume.

The proliferation of poster art from the 1880s to the First World War coincided with improved printing techniques and better distribution, which was aided by the ever-growing transport system. Competition in the market place meant that advertisers had to become canny; by the 1920s graphic designers realized that their art needed to achieve instant visual impact and brand recognition.

MOVEMENT

Art Nouveau

SIMILAR WORKS

Job by Alphonse Mucha, 1897

MEDIUM

Poster

Privat Livemont *Born* 1861 Schaerbeek, Brussels

Died 1936

Cézanne, Paul

Still Life with Apples, 1893–94

Courtesy of Private Collection/Bridgeman Art Gallery/Christie's Images

A French painter, Cézanne was a leading member of the Post-Impressionists. Born in Aix-en-Provence, the son of a banker, Cézanne's prosperous background enabled him to endure the long struggle for recognition. He studied in Paris, where he met the future members of the Impressionist circle, although his own work at this time was full of violent, Romantic imagery. Cézanne did not mix easily with the group; he was withdrawn, suspicious and prey to sudden rages. Gradually, with Pissarro's encouragement, he tried *plein-air* painting and participated at two of the Impressionist exhibitions. But, in art as in life, Cézanne was a solitary figure and he soon found the principles of the movement too restricting.

After his father's death in 1886, Cézanne returned to Aix, where he brought his style to maturity. His aim was to produce 'constructions after nature'. He followed the Impressionist practice of painting outdoors but, instead of the transient effects which they sought, he tried to capture the underlying geometry of the natural world. This was to make him a fertile source of inspiration for the Cubists.

MOVEMENT

Post-Impressionism

OTHER WORKS

Mont Sainte-Victoire; Apples and Oranges; The Card Players

INFLUENCES

Delacroix, Courbet, Pissarro

Paul Cézanne *Born* 1839 France

Died 1906

Munch, Edvard

The Scream, 1893

Edvard Munch studied in Christiania (now Oslo) and travelled in Germany, Italy and France before settling in Oslo. During his time in Paris (1908) he came under the influence of Gauguin and had immense sympathy for Van Gogh due to the bouts of mental illness from which both suffered. In fact, this would have a profound effect on the development of Munch as an artist and explains the extraordinary passion that pervades his work. Life, love and death are the themes that he endlessly explored in his paintings, rendered in an Expressionist symbolic style. His use of swirling lines and strident colours emphasize the angst that lies behind his paintings. He also produced etchings, lithographs and woodcut engravings which influenced the German artists of the movement known as Die Brücke.

MOVEMENT

Expressionism

OTHER WORKS

Puberty, The Dance of Life; The Madonna; Ashes

INFLUENCES

Gauguin, Van Gogh

Edvard Munch *Born* 1863 Loten, Norway

Died 1944

Gauguin, Paul
Nave Nave Moe, 1894

Courtesy of Hermitage, St Petersburg/Bridgeman/Christie's Images

Although he was born in Paris, Gauguin spent his early childhood in Peru, returning to France in 1855. He worked for a time as a stockbroker, painting only as a hobby, until the stock market crash of 1882 prompted a dramatic change of career. His first pictures were in the Impressionist style, influenced in particular by his friend, Camille Pissarro. Increasingly, though, Gauguin became dissatisfied with the purely visual emphasis of the movement, and tried to introduce a greater degree of symbolism and spirituality into his work. Inspired by Japanese prints, he also developed a new style, coupling bold splashes of bright, unmixed colour with simplified, linear designs. At the same time, haunted by memories of his Peruvian childhood, Gauguin developed a growing fascination for exotic and primitive cultures. Initially, he was able to satisfy this need in Brittany where, inspired by the region's distinctive Celtic traditions, he produced *The Vision after the Sermon*, his first great masterpiece. Then in 1891, he moved to the French colony of Tahiti. Dogged by poverty and ill health, he spent most of his later life in this area producing the paintings for which he is best known today.

MOVEMENTS
Post-Impressionism/Impressionism/Symbolism

OTHER WORKS
Where Do We Come From? What Are We? Where Are We Going To?

INFLUENCES
Camille Pissarro, Emile Bernard, Vincent Van Gogh

Paul Gauguin *Born* 1848 Paris, France
Died 1903

Sickert, Walter

L'Hotel Royal Dieppe, c. 1894

Born in Munich, Bavaria, Walter Richard Sickert was the son of the painter Oswald Adalbert Sickert and grandson of the painter and lithographer Johannes Sickert. With such an artistic pedigree it was almost inevitable that he should follow the family tradition. In 1868 his parents moved to London, where he later studied at the Slade School of Art and took lessons from Whistler, whose limited tonal range is reflected in much of Sickert's work. On the advice of Degas – whom he met while studying in Paris – he made detailed preliminary drawings for his paintings rather than paint from life. As a youth, Sickert had been an actor and he had a lifelong interest in the theater, reflected in many of his paintings. He was a competent all-rounder, painting portraits, rather seedy genre subjects and murky landscapes, and as a teacher he wielded enormous influence on the British artists of the early twentieth century.

MOVEMENT

British Impressionism

OTHER WORKS

Mornington Crescent Nude; La Hollandaise Nude

INFLUENCES

James McNeill Whistler, Degas

Sickert, Walter *Born 1860 Munich, Germany*

Died 1942

Beardsley, Aubrey

Isolde, illustration from *The Studio*, 1895

© Private Collection, The Stapleton Collection/www.bridgeman.co.uk

Aubrey Beardsley had shown a talent for drawing from an early age. As an adult his short-lived career was meteoric; he was catapulted to fame by his illustrations for magazines such as *The Studio* and *The Yellow Book*. The young man gained notoriety and adulation in equal measure before his premature death at the age of 26.

The work of this illustrator and artist pulls together many themes, styles and techniques of his era and earlier. Of all of the influences, Japanese woodcuts, which Beardsley collected, are possibly the most important. The overall effect, however, was to produce a highly innovative body of work. His stark use of black and white, his evocative lines and his tendency towards the erotic were considered outrageous and decadent by many. The effect and influence of his work is now regarded as being enormous, and unfulfilled predictions by fellow artists, such as Edward Burne-Jones, that he would 'most assuredly paint very good and beautiful pictures' are poignant. Aware that he was dying, Beardsley converted to Catholicism and begged that his obscene pictures be destroyed; fortunately for us, they were not.

MOVEMENT

Aestheticism/Art Nouveau

OTHER WORKS

The Dreamer

MEDIUM

Colour lithograph

Aubrey Beardsley *Born* 1872 Brighton, England

Died 1898

Mucha, Alphonse

La Danse

Alphonse Mucha's patron for a number of years was the brilliant French actress, Sarah Bernhardt (1874–1934). She was also an astute businesswoman who recognized Mucha's unique talent. His posters were instantly eye-catching, captivating and beautiful; all qualities that could be attributed to Bernhardt. It is interesting to note that while many Art Nouveau images of women were almost ethereal and at least stylized, there were very occasionally real women, the *femmes nouvelles* of the era, behind the fakes.

Sarah Bernhardt was one of two entertainers who came to embody the Art Nouveau woman for many people: Loïe Fuller (1862–1928) was the other. Fuller was an American dancer who came to Paris's Folies Bergère in 1892 and became the darling of the Parisian avant-garde. She had choreographed a divine dance using layers of Chinese silk that billowed and undulated as she moved. Fuller danced on a glass floor that was lit from below, causing the veils of fabric to change colour as they flowed evocatively. Fuller was adored by Symbolist artists and writers and they tried to capture the effect that her visual display had had on them.

MOVEMENT

Art Nouveau

OTHER WORK S

Poster of *Les Saisons*, 1900

MEDIUM

Poster

Alphonse Mucha *Born* 1860 Ivancice, Moravia

Died 1939

Vuillard, Edouard

Causerie chez les Fontaines

Jean Edouard Vuillard studied at the Académie Julien in Paris and shared a studio with Pierre Bonnard. Both artists were inspired by Sérusier's theories derived from the works of Gauguin and became founder members of Les Nabis in 1889. Vuillard was also influenced by the fashion for Japanese prints and this was reflected in his paintings of flowers and domestic interiors, executed with a keen sense of tone, colour and light. He was also a prolific designer of textiles, wallpaper and decorative features for public buildings. His paintings of cozy domestic subjects show a tremendous feeling for texture and patterning, a skill he picked up from his mother who was a dressmaker. The bolts of brightly coloured cloth that surrounded him as a child found an echo in his own textile designs. His later paintings were more naturalistic, aided by photography, which he employed to capture the fleeting moment.

MOVEMENT

Les Nabis

OTHER WORKS

Femme Lisant; Le Soir; Two Schoolboys; Mother and Child

INFLUENCES

Paul Sérusier, Gauguin

Edouard Vuillard *Born* 1868 Cuiseaux, France

Died 1940

Modersohn-Becker, Paula

Mother and Child, 1903

© Hamburg Kunsthalle, Hamburg, Germany/www.bridgeman.co.uk

Paula Becker was first formed creatively by her time at Worpswede, an artists' colony outside Bremen, from 1898, and by her marriage there to fellow artist Otto Modersohn. The resulting painter was well-behaved, creating conservative – even rather sentimental – landscapes and portraits; appealing enough, but never the least bit surprising, still less unsettling. All this was to change, partly in response to the works of Vincent Van Gogh (1853–90) and Paul Gauguin (1848–1903) seen during a series of visits to Paris at the start of the century, and partly through her conversations with poet Rainer Maria Rilke (1875–1926), whose muse she became. Mostly, however, the breakthrough was her own resolution that she would hold fast to her 'personal vision'. Emotional integrity was at the centre of her work.

Determination is as much a feature of the mother here as it seems to have been of Paula: maternal love is matter of fact, and as tough as it is tender. No ethereal Madonna, this woman is a figure of physical strength and fierce protectiveness, but she still suggests a certain serenity and contentment. Tragically, the artist herself died in the aftermath of childbirth.

MOVEMENT

Expressionism

SIMILAR WORKS

Alexei Jawlensky, *Head*, c. 1910

MEDIUM

Oil on canvas

Paula Modersohn-Becker *Born* 1876 Dresden, Germany

Died 1907

Rackham, Arthur

The Meeting of Oberon and Titania, 1905

Rackham produced this sparkling scene for the 1908 edition of *A Midsummer Night's Dream*, although in the end it was not used in the final version of the book. It depicts precisely the same episode that Paton had depicted in 1849, underlining the seismic changes that had taken place in the field of fairy painting during the intervening years. With their fine clothes and their regal airs, Rackham's royal couple are the stuff of pantomimes and fairy tales, quite unlike the nude, Classical figures of Paton. More significantly his fairies are well-mannered children, content to hold lanterns and carry their masters' trains, while Paton's creatures cavort lustily in the undergrowth.

Shakespeare derived his fairies from a number of different sources. Oberon stems from *Huon of Bordeaux*, a thirteenth-century romance that was first translated into English by Lord Berners (*c.* 1469–1533). In this, Huon performs a number of seemingly impossible tasks, with the magical assistance of the fairy king. Titania, meanwhile, came from a Classical source. Ovid (43 BC–AD 17) had used the name to describe a number of female woodland spirits who were descended from the Titans, an ancient race of Greek gods. Puck, or Robin Goodfellow, was well known from English folklore, but Shakespeare may have found additional information in Reginald Scot's (*c.* 1538–99) *Discoverie of Witchcraft* (1584).

MOVEMENT

Art Nouveau

SIMILAR WORKS

Come Unto These Yellow Sands by Thomas Maybank

MEDIUM

Pen, ink and watercolour

Arthur Rackham *Born* 1867 London, England

Died 1939

Mackintosh, Charles Rennie

The Wassail (detail), 1900

The Wassail is a watercolour completed by Charles Rennie Mackintosh for a series of three gesso (bas-relief in plaster of Paris, or gypsum) panels for the Ladies' Luncheon Room at the Ingram Street Tea Rooms in Glasgow. The owner of the tea rooms, Catherine Cranston, was a supporter of the Temperance movement and opened a series of tea rooms to provide women, in particular, with a meeting place that was free of alcohol. Margaret Macdonald (1864–1933) worked with her husband on many of his design and architectural projects and there is a strong similarity between the gesso panels, attributed to Mackintosh, and work attributed to Macdonald. The architect Edwin Luytens (1869–1944) described the tea rooms as 'all very elaborately simple'.

The women in the drawings are typically elongated, almost 'pod-like'. The Glasgow style often incorporated Symbolism, a popular idiom for Art Nouveau. Symbolism concentrates on a world that exists beyond the obvious and uses symbols and images to depict the abstract, such as the exotic, erotic, occult and spiritual. The blood-red flowers were a favourite symbol for Mackintosh and Macdonald: they symbolize the fertility of women.

MOVEMENT

Art Nouveau

OTHER WORKS

Wall panels from Buchanan Street Tea Rooms

MEDIUM

Watercolour and pencil on paper

Charles Rennie Mackintosh *Born* 1868 Glasgow, Scotland

Died 1928

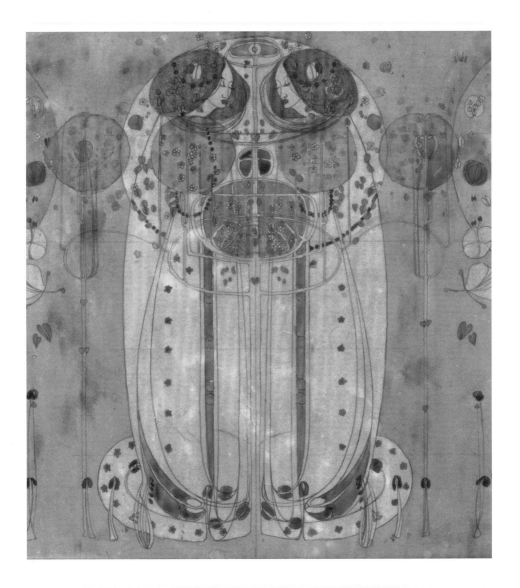

Klimt, Gustav

Emilie Floege

Gustav Klimt's father was a gold and silver engraver, a labour that doubtless had some effect on Klimt who later decorated his work with these precious metals. The family lived in a Viennese suburb and Klimt received a formal education in art at the Vienna School of Decorative Arts, specializing in murals. Gustav Klimt's talents were immediately spotted and he received commissions while still at college. He decorated two public buildings in Vienna: the Burgtheater and the Kunsthistorisches Museum, working in collaboration with his brother and a friend. By the age of 30 Klimt was a renowned and successful artist.

In 1893 Klimt received a commission to paint murals for a new university building. The ceiling paintings received some criticism from the rationalist, traditional quarters, for Klimt was beginning his experimental phase of art with intensive, creative energy. Three more commissions from the university caused uproar when they were unveiled (they were later destroyed by the Nazis). Packed with sensuality, Symbolist and Aesthetic ideology, Klimt's art could only find favour with those who understood his profound and challenging vision.

MOVEMENT

Secession

OTHER WORKS

Portrait of the Baroness Elizabeth Bachofen-Echt; The Kiss

MEDIUM

Oil on canvas

Gustav Klimt *Born* 1862 Vienna, Austria

Died 1918

Cowper, Frank Cadogan

Francis of Assisi and the Heavenly Melody, 1902

St Francis of Assisi (1182–1226) was famed during his lifetime as the founder of the Franciscan order of mendicant friars. He is shown wearing their brown habit in this picture, together with the traditional girdle. This has three knots representing the friar's triple vow of poverty, chastity and obedience. The colourful details of Francis's life were portrayed by many artists, most notably Giotto (*c.* 1270–1327), and they often chose to focus on the saint's affinity with birds and animals. These were said to become tame in his presence. He is also said to have preached sermons to the birds, likening their song to the music of heavenly choirs. In one of his addresses he urged them to praise God for his blessings, at which point the birds took off, flying into the formation of a cross.

Cowper is sometimes described as the last of the Pre-Raphaelites. He studied at the St John's Wood Art School and the Royal Academy before travelling to Italy. From the outset, Cowper's approach was remarkable for its meticulous attention to detail. Before embarking on this painting, for example, he was determined to visit Assisi to ensure that the picture's setting looked authentic.

MOVEMENT

Pre-Raphaelite

SIMILAR WORKS

The Boer War by John Byam Shaw, 1900

MEDIUM

Oil on canvas

Frank Cadogan Cowper *Born* 1877 Wicken, England

Died 1958

Hughes, Edward Robert

Midsummer Eve, 1908

During the later stages of the nineteenth century, a growing number of artists showed humans coming into contact with fairies. These encounters were usually friendly, unlike the earlier examples in folk tales or fairy literature where the humans were invariably punished for intruding on the privacy of the tiny creatures. This painting has some affinities with *The Introduction* by Eleanor Fortescue Brickdale (1871–1945), although Hughes's picture is far more atmospheric. This is largely due to the ambiguity, which arises from the uncertain link between the woman and the fairies. At first glance she appears to be human, but it is quite possible that she is meant to be some form of wood nymph. Her bare feet confirm that she is no casual passer-by, while the rapturous welcome she receives within the fairy ring is most uncharacteristic. Moreover, the flowers that adorn her dress and hair offer the suggestion that she may herself be a woodland creature. Most telling of all is the pipe that dangles from her side. From this it can be deduced that the girl has drawn the fairies to her by playing their magical music on her instrument.

MOVEMENT

Fairy Art/Pre-Raphaelite

SIMILAR WORKS

The White Knight by Walter Crane, 1870

The Lover's World by Eleanor Fortescue Brickdale, 1905

MEDIUM

Watercolour and body colour

Edward Robert Hughes *Born* 1849 London, England

Died 1914

Waterhouse, John William

The Annunciation, 1914

The Pre-Raphaelites and their successors tried to instil a greater sense of realism into their religious pictures. In doing so they were following the advice of the critic, John Ruskin (1819–1900), who urged painters to portray the virgin as 'a simple Jewish girl', rather than 'a graceful princess crowned with gems'.

Waterhouse's remarkable version of the subject certainly breathed new life into the theme, avoiding many of the old clichés. He portrays the virgin as a young woman rather than a sacred icon. Her pose is very natural, reflecting her obvious surprise at seeing an angel appear out of nowhere. The setting is presented in an equally novel fashion, even though it manages to include several of the customary symbols. Traditionally the virgin is kneeling at a *prie-dieu* when Gabriel arrives. On it there is a text from the Old Testament prophesying the coming of the Saviour. According to St Bernard this came from Isaiah: 'Behold a virgin shall conceive, and bear a son' (Isaiah VII:14). Often, as here, there is a distaff (a stick for spinning thread) by the virgin's side. This alludes to the legend that Mary was raised at the Temple in Jerusalem, where she made vestments for the priests.

MOVEMENT

Pre-Raphaelite

SIMILAR WORKS

The Nativity by Dorothy Webster Hawksley

John William Waterhouse *Born* 1849 Rome, Italy

Died 1917

The Modern Age

1900–present

Derain, André

Self Portrait with a Cap, c. 1905

André Derain was a friend of Henri Matisse, and had for a time shared a studio with Maurice de Vlaminck, so it was inevitable that he should have been one of the founding Fauves. A work like this one reminds us that, however 'wild' their palette and however untamed their technique, the Fauves were amiability itself in their relationship with their viewer, and never interested in attacking anything other than worn out convention.

With all its superficial outlandishness, this self-portrait is a work of genuine psychological depth: there is real warmth and intelligence in the expression of the artist-subject. Yet Derain does not assault us emotionally in the way the Expressionists would do: the impression we have is of a man at ease with himself and with his world. And, for that matter, with his art: this is a wonderfully accomplished work — eccentric in its parts, perhaps, but utterly convincing as a whole. The counterpointing of outline and surface texture, the play of contrasting colours, of shadow and sun, add up to an extraordinarily fresh and yet endlessly absorbing work of art.

MOVEMENT

Fauvism

SIMILAR WORKS

Georges Rouault, *Nude with Raised Arm*, 1906

MEDIUM

Oil on canvas

André Derain *Born* 1880 near Paris, France

Died 1954

Dufy, Raoul

The Three Umbrellas, 1906

Raoul Dufy had already achieved some standing as an Impressionist painter when, in 1906, he underwent a Road-to-Damascus conversion. The occasion of this great event was his first encounter with Henri Matisse's (1868–1954) *Luxe, Calme et Volupté* ('Luxury, calm and delight', a phrase from a Baudelaire poem). Matisse's masterpiece, one of the culminating works of his Neo-Impressionist period, had many of the characteristics of what would come to be known as 'Fauvist' painting. It was, Dufy marvelled, a 'miracle of creative imagination in colour and line', and colour and line became the main preoccupations of his own 'creative imagination' in his work thereafter. As an Impressionist, Dufy would have attempted a quasi-photographic reproduction of this riverside scene: Impressionism was a highly realistic school, despite its superficial messiness. Here, however, the colours and curves of the umbrellas become the centre of a swirling semi-abstract symphony in paint; the human forms are not only secondary, but almost disembodied, just parts of the pattern. 'Colours became charges of dynamite ... Everything could be raised above the real ...', as André Derain would remark later of the Fauvist school.

MOVEMENT

Fauvism

SIMILAR WORKS

André Derain, *London: St Paul's Cathedral Seen from the Thames*, 1906

MEDIUM

Oil on canvas

Raoul Dufy *Born* 1877 Le Havre, France

Died 1953.

Matisse, Henri

Still Life with 'La Danse', 1909

'What I am after, above all, is expression,' wrote Henri Matisse in 1908, and he set out to achieve this chiefly through his use of colour. But making a living was important too, as we see in the extraordinary piece of product placement which sees *La Danse*, an earlier work by Matisse, appearing, as though incidentally, in the background of his scene. The self-advertisement is a reminder of how large the market loomed in the painter's life in an art world in which private collectors, rather than ecclesiastical or aristocratic patrons, had come to dominate. Eager to possess the latest thing, and where possible to upstage one another with the originality and daring of the works they bought, such collectors had a significant (if unquantifiable) influence on the development of twentieth-century art.

Matisse was famously a leading light in the circle of Parisian painters known as *les fauves* ('wild beasts'), but the label obscures as much as it illuminates. The wildness certainly comes across here in a palette that assaults the visual sense, and in the paradox of a 'still life' whose surging energy makes it seem anything but still.

MOVEMENT

Fauvism

SIMILAR WORKS

Raoul Dufy, *Still Life with Bananas, c.* 1909

MEDIUM

Oil on canvas

Henri Matisse *Born* 1869 Picardy, France

Died 1954

Münter, Gabriele

Village Street in Winter, 1911

A student of Wassily Kandinsky (1866–1944) and for many years his lover (although never his artistic emulator), Gabriele Münter became a leading light of the *Neue Künstlervereinigung München* ('New Artists' Association of Munich' or NKV). Founded in 1909, the NKV was not strictly speaking a school or movement: its purpose was to provide a venue for exhibiting works that fell foul of the city's highly conservative artistic establishment. Certain shared values did emerge, however. In particular the French Fauves had a major impact, seen in this cityscape, with its out-of-kilter structures and crazy colour scheme. Münter's bold strokes and childlike composition could hardly have contrasted more starkly with the elegant sophistication and subtle tones of *Jugendstil*, the German version of Art Nouveau, still in vogue. Respectable citizens flocked to NKV exhibitions just to register contempt – one dealer had to wipe the spit from the canvases every night. Ironically, though, the movement would be a casualty of its own conservatism. When one of his pictures was rejected for exhibition in 1911, Kandinsky formed the rival *Der Blaue Reiter* ('Blue Rider') group, which effectively eclipsed it.

MOVEMENT

Neue Künstlervereinigung München

SIMILAR WORKS

Alexei von Jawlensky, *Landscape with Red Roof*, c. 1911

MEDIUM

Oil on canvas

Gabriele Münter *Born* 1877 Berlin, Germany

Died 1962

Macke, August
Woman in a Green Jacket, 1913

© Ludwig Museum, Cologne, Germany/www.bridgeman.co.uk

'Incomprehensible ideas have comprehensible forms ...', wrote August Macke in 1912 in a contribution to the almanac of the *Der Blaue Reiter* movement. 'The senses are our bridge between the incomprehensible and the comprehensible...', he continued: 'Forms are powerful expressions of powerful life.' Or so, at least they should be: Macke went on to deplore the divorce between increasingly empty, prettified forms in western art, and the deep emotional wellsprings of human life. He professed himself astonished, as well as disgusted, at the banishment of 'primitive' art to the ethnographical museum. European artists should recover the savage's connection with the elemental, he insisted.

Twentieth-century art was never to be short of such radical rallying cries, of course, and often the bigger the declaration the smaller the achievement. Yet there is no disputing the fact that Macke was accessing profound emotions in his art, and doing so, as he claimed, through works of immense simplicity. Despite his rhetoric he created some of German Expressionism's least portentous works: it is no surprise to find that he was greatly influenced by French models, such as the paintings of the Fauves.

MOVEMENT

Der Blaue Reiter/Expressionism

SIMILAR WORKS

Alexei von Jawlensky, *Seated Woman*, 1911

MEDIUM

Oil on canvas

August Macke *Born* 1887 Westphalia, Germany

Died 1914

Kandinsky, Wassily
Composition No. 7, 1913

'An empty canvas, apparently really empty, that says nothing and is without significance. Almost dull, in fact. In reality, however, crammed with thousands of undertone tensions and full of expectancy. Slightly apprehensive lest it should be outraged. Yet docile enough. Ready to do what is required of it, and only asking for consideration ... An empty canvas is a living wonder.' Thus wrote the great Expressionist Wassily Kandinsky, towards the end of his extraordinary career in 1937. For him wonder was the great theme of art: art was a spiritual, mystical experience, both in creation and contemplation. He and his fellow founders of *Der Blaue Reiter* shared comparatively little in terms of technique, but were united by a sense that the artist should have free rein to find whatever form suited his or her need for self-expression. In his case that would eventually mean abstraction, rich and colourful, although in the movement's early years he still offered tantalizing, semi-figurative forms. The sense of wonder was the same, however, as more crowded canvases were surely never seen; every space seemingly a painting waiting to happen.

MOVEMENT

Der Blaue Reiter/Expressionism

SIMILAR WORKS

Franz Marc, *The Unfortunate Land of Tyrol*, 1913

MEDIUM

Oil on canvas

Wassily Kandinsky *Born* 1866 Moscow, Russia

Died 1944

de Chirico, Giorgio

The Mystery and Melancholy of a Street, 1914

'We who understand the signs of the metaphysical alphabet know what joys and sorrows are hidden within a portico, the angle of a street.' Giorgio de Chirico built a city of symbols in his art. By tradition emblems of order and regularity, the 'classical' arches, columns and statues he favoured in his work hinted ironically at the limits of human reason and the irreducible unknown that lay beyond. It was up to art to explore this realm, at least implicitly, he felt. Accordingly, around 1913, he formulated the philosophy of his *Pittura Metafisica* ('Metaphysical Painting'). 'To become truly immortal,' he wrote, 'a work of art must escape all human limits: logic and common sense will only interfere.' Carlo Carrà promptly consigned his Futurism to the past in his eagerness to follow him, although the two would part company again a few years later.

The Mystery and Melancholy of a Street is an utterly extraordinary work, inexpressibly haunting and yet its compositional components are strikingly familiar. Walking the frontier between figure and shadow, physical reality and thought, it offers a scary, uplifting glimpse into infinite space.

MOVEMENT

Pittura Metafisica

SIMILAR WORKS

Alexei von Jawlensky, *Paesaggio*, 1911

MEDIUM

Oil on canvas

Giorgio de Chirico *Born* 1888 Volo, Greece, 1888

Died 1978

Braque, Georges
Man with a Guitar, 1914

Georges Braque was born in France, close to one of the centres of the Impressionist movement. When he was 15, Braque attended evening classes at Le Havre Academy of Fine Arts where he mastered the skills, techniques and materials necessary to pursue his dream of becoming a professional artist. After completing his military training, Braque continued his art studies at a private Parisian academy. Braque's early works show the influence of the Impressionist painters but by 1905, after seeing Fauvist works at the Paris *Salon d'Automne*, he had begun to develop his own style. The controversial Fauvists ('Les Fauves', literally 'the wild beasts') were led by Henri Matisse (1869–1954) and they painted from nature, like the Impressionists, but employed explosions of colour to create movement, emotion and a sense of space.

In 1907 Braque was introduced to Pablo Picasso. The two men worked closely together for the next few years and through their collaboration invented Cubism. Although Cubism and Art Deco appear diametrically opposed, they both sought inspiration from many of the same sources, together forging much of the art and design of the early twentieth century and beyond.

MOVEMENT

Cubism

SIMILAR WORKS

L'Estaque by Braque, 1908

Des Demoiselles d'Avignon by Pablo Picasso, 1907

MEDIUM

Oil on canvas

Georges Braque *Born* 1882 Argenteuil, France

Died 1963

Gris, Juan

Breakfast, 1915

© Musée National d'Art Moderne, Centre Pompidou, Paris, France, Peter Willi/www.bridgeman.co.uk

Paradoxical, even perverse in its workings, Cubism did more than any other movement to free modern painting from the mimetic responsibilities of old. It defied the two-dimensionality of the canvas, it dismantled every scene into its component planes, and it made items square so that they could be exhibited 'in the round'.

The vogue for Cubism swept Paris in the decade before the First World War. For its greatest practitioners, though, it was far more than a fashion. Gertrude Stein, the émigrée American writer and champion of all things avant-garde, noted that to Juan Gris in particular Cubism was 'a religion'. She meant in part that Gris was more at pains than most to follow through a theory of aesthetics in his work, and to systematize what for others might be no more than an ad hoc device or posture. 'Truth is beyond any realism,' he said, 'and the appearance of things should not be confused with their essence.' Stein also put a finger on something clearly evidenced in this remarkably atmospheric still life: the profound spirituality underlying what might seem no more than a geometrical game.

MOVEMENT

Cubism

SIMILAR WORKS

Pablo Picasso, *Still Life with Chair-Caning*, 1912

MEDIUM

Oil on canvas

Juan Gris *Born* 1887 Madrid, Spain

Died 1927

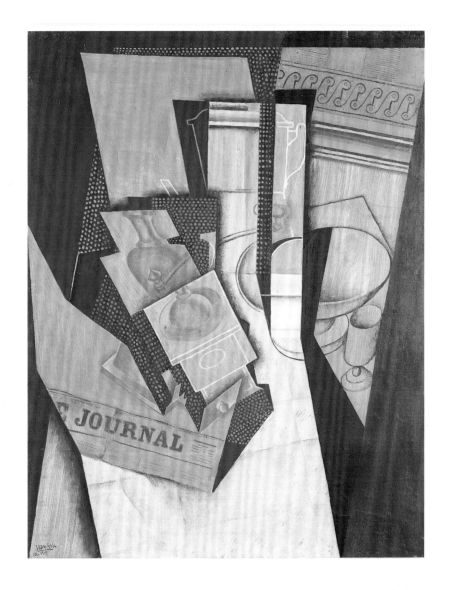

Delaunay, Sonia

Ses Peintures, Ses Objets, Ses Tissus Simultanes, Ses Modes: Twenty Color Plates c. 1912–25

Courtesy of Christie's Images Ltd/© L & M Services B. V. Amsterdam 2005/0512

The allocation of artists to 'schools' or 'movements' is often an arbitrary convenience as most are individualists by nature. Moreover, their work changes and develops as they themselves grow older and as influences come crowding in upon their lives, so an energetic artist may belong to several schools or none in the course of a career. Sonia Delaunay is a good example: she has gone down in art history as an Orphist, a justifiable categorization as far as it goes. She was the wife of Robert Delaunay (1885–1941), the movement's leader, and his influence is evident here. Yet if she had married the man, she certainly had not married his movement. Earlier in the century, Sonia had been strongly influenced by the Fauves, an influence she was obviously slow to put aside. Orphism was generally less precisely defined than is often assumed, hence the peripheral involvement of avowed Cubists such as Francis Picabia (1879–1953). An artist like Sonia Delaunay would ultimately always remain her own woman with her own ideas.

MOVEMENT

Orphism

MEDIUM

Pochoir

Sonia Delaunay *Born* 1885 Ukraine, Russia

Died 1979

1915

Sonia Delaunay

Sonia Delaunay   7

Duchamp, Marcel

L.H.O.O.Q, Mona Lisa with a Moustache, 1919/1930

During the second half of 1919, Marcel Duchamp returned to Paris, making contact again with members of the Parisian avant-garde, particularly the Dadaists around André Breton and Paul Eluard (1895–1952). Although there for only six months he made one of the most famous Dada statements by inscribing a reproduction of Leonardo da Vinci's *Mona Lisa* with the letters 'L.H.O.O.Q' and drawing a moustache on her face. The letters when spelt out in French read phonetically as *Elle a chaud au cul*, which translates as 'She's got a hot arse'.

This work constitutes an 'assisted' ready-made in which Duchamp would purchase an everyday item and re-appropriate its use as an art work, either by redefining its nomenclature or defacing it in some way as in the *Mona Lisa*. During the period of his exile in New York, Duchamp made a number of works that he defined as 'ready-mades' such as *In Advance of a Broken Arm*, in which he propped a snow shovel against the wall, and the 'assisted' *50cc of Paris Air* in which he presented an empty glass ampoule that he had purchased in Paris. Duchamp's work at this time was very radical and had a considerable influence on the artists of the 1960s such as Piero Manzoni (1933–1963).

MOVEMENT

Dada

SIMILAR WORKS

Francis Picabia, *Dada Portrait*, 1920

MEDIUM

Ready-made postcard and pencil

Marcel Duchamp *Born* 1887 Blainville-Crevon, France

Died 1968

Léger, Fernand

The Pilot, 1920

Having been a draughtsman in an architects' practice, Fernand Léger took up painting around 1900, and from 1909 he became an enthusiastic but unorthodox Cubist. His earlier apprenticeship perhaps informed his interest in geometrical structures, which became increasingly prominent in his work. By the time he painted this one, it was teetering on the very brink of abstraction, yet this is still just about recognizable as representational work. Characteristically it gives us a sense not only of the pilot, but also of his aeroplane, with its propeller, its controls and internal workings. Léger's fascination with all things mechanical echoes that of the Italian Futurists and leads to similarities between their works, but his interest was altogether different. In his lecture, published in 1924, 'The Aesthetic of the Machine', he makes it clear that the appeal of technology lies not in its power and ferocity, but in the fact that it belongs to the domain of the everyday into which aesthetics has not hitherto ventured much. 'Beauty is everywhere,' he says, 'in the arrangement of your pots and pans, on the white wall of your kitchen, more perhaps than in your eighteenth-century salon or in the official museum.'

MOVEMENT

Cubism

SIMILAR WORKS

Albert Gleizes, *Portrait of a Young Man*, c. 1910

MEDIUM

Oil on canvas

Fernand Léger *Born* 1881 Argentan, France

Died 1955

Klee, Paul

The Lamb, 1920

In the same year in which he created this animal figure, Paul Klee published his *Creative Credo*: 'Art does not reproduce the visible; rather, it makes visible', it said. 'A tendency towards the abstract is inherent in linear expression: graphic imagery being confined to outlines has a fairy-like quality and at the same time can achieve great precision.'

A work such as this one evidently exploits this twofold quality, representational form and abstract background each counterpointing and complementing one another. Colour is counterpointed too: by early training as an etching specialist, Klee had come to colour relatively late in his artistic development. He sensed its importance in the works of his friend and mentor Wassily Kandinsky (1886–1944), and in 1910 recorded his ambition to be able to improvise freely on the 'keyboard of adjacent pots of paint'. The breakthrough came in the sunshine of Tunisia, where he went with August Macke and Louis Moilliet in 1914. 'Colour has got me', he wrote. 'I don't need to run after it. It's got me forever, I know it. That is the meaning of this happy hour: colour and I are one. I am a painter.'

MOVEMENT

Der Blaue Reiter/Expressionism

SIMILAR WORKS

Franz Marc, *Tiger*, 1912

MEDIUM

Watercolour

Paul Klee *Born* 1879 Münchenbuchsee, Switzerland

Died 1940

Schwitters, Kurt

Merzzeichnung 229, 1921

The use of collage was adapted from the Cubists, particularly Pablo Picasso (1881–1973) and Georges Braque (1882–1963), whose art the Dadaists now considered bourgeois rather than avant-garde. Apart from Max Ernst (1891–1976) the greatest exponent of the use of collage for Dada was Kurt Schwitters, who turned his back on Expressionist painting after meeting Hans Arp (1887–1966) and became the sole representative of Dada in Hanover. His own style of collage, which he called *Merz*, used detritus collected from the street, including bus tickets, tin lids and cigarette stubs. It is often described as Abstract Assemblage. Schwitters was like all modern artists exploring Charles Baudelaire's ideas of modernity expressed half a century before as, 'the ephemeral, the fugitive, the contingent, the one half of art whose other half is the eternal and immutable'.

His use of detritus as collage, or as he called it *Merzbild* and its veneration as a medium alongside that of paint, was to be an important contribution to the post-Second World War generation of Dadaists in America, such as Robert Rauschenberg (b. 1925) and Jasper Johns (b. 1930) who paved the way for the subsequent generation of Pop Art.

MOVEMENT

Dada

SIMILAR WORKS

Max Ernst, *Massacre of the Innocents*, 1921

MEDIUM

Paper and textile collage on card

Kurt Schwitters *Born* 1887 Hanover, Germany

Died 1948

Ernst, Max
Celebes, 1921

Like many European artists Max Ernst was disillusioned with bourgeois values following the futility of the First World War. After his service in the German Army he became the leader of the circle of Dada artists, which included Hans Arp, in Cologne. In 1920 he organized one of the most famous Dada exhibitions, in a restaurant in which visitors entered through the lavatories and were invited to break the exhibits with axes if they wanted. Then from 1922 he joined the Parisian group under the leadership of André Breton (1896–1966). Prior to his involvement in the Surrealist movement after 1924, Ernst painted a number of works that anticipate Surrealism while still reflecting the irony of Dadaism – for example, *Celebes*, and his depiction of a nonsense German poem whose opening line is 'The elephant from Celebes has sticky yellow bottom grease...'. In this painting Ernst has used his earlier university studies in psychology and philosophy, in which he became familiar with the writings of Friedrich Nietzsche (1844–1900) and Sigmund Freud (1856–1939), to provide the basis for a pictorial exploration of the irrational subconscious.

MOVEMENT

Dada/proto-Surrealism

SIMILAR WORKS

Francis Picabia, *Amorous Procession*, 1917

MEDIUM

Oil on canvas

Max Ernst *Born* 1891 Brühl, Germany

Died 1976

Bayer, Herbert

Sheet Music, 1921

Architect Walter Gropius (1883–1969) established the Bauhaus ('House for Building') in Weimar, Germany, in 1919. His aim was to bring artistic principles to bear on the design and construction of everything from buildings to lamps and to give the artist a real function in society. The emphasis was on 'applied' art, then, but 'pure' painting had its place: the Bauhaus' first director of art was Wassily Kandinsky (1866–1944), Bayer's master and later his teaching colleague at the Bauhaus.

Along with the great works of abstraction for which he is now famous, Kandinsky had produced a profoundly influential book, *Concerning the Spiritual in Modern Art* (1911). It proposed a mystic vision of art, bringing music and painting together to promote a 'spiritual change' in those who experienced it, touching them at a level beyond that of any superficial 'beauty'. Such an art already existed, Kandinsky suggested, in the 'atonal' music of Arnold Schoenburg; a comparable art would codify colours as 'vibrations of the soul'. Suggestions of such a mystic order (and allusions to musical instruments and notation) can clearly be seen in Bayer's composition.

MOVEMENT

Bauhaus

SIMILAR WORKS

Paul Klee, *Tänzerpaar*, 1923

MEDIUM

Watercolour and pencil on paper

Herbert Bayer *Born* 1900 Haag, Austria

Died 1985

Moholy-Nagy, László
Architektur I, 1922

Courtesy of The Nicolas M. Salgo Collection, USA/www.bridgeman.co.uk/© DACS 2005

'Hungarian Activism' was briefly the particular form in which the Modernist wave hit Hungary, a response to Cubism, Expressionism, Futurism and all the other new schools. As in Russia, the embrace of the new in art went along with specifically socialist political ideals. The movement was led by Lajos Kassák, who published a famous journal, *MA* ('Today'). Its intention according to a contributor was, 'not ... to establish a new school of art but a completely new conception of art and the world'.

In 1919 it looked as though he might just get his way: a Soviet Republic was proclaimed in Hungary, but it collapsed completely within four months of its creation and many artists were compelled to go into exile. Perhaps the movement's most important talent, Moholy-Nagy was among them. At first he set up in Vienna, then in 1921 he went to Berlin, but he was moving on both geographically and artistically all the time. Within a year of creating this work he would be in Weimar, a master at the Bauhaus, where he would at least help bring about 'a new conception of art'.

MOVEMENT
Hungarian Activism/Constructivism/Bauhaus

SIMILAR WORKS
Lajos Kassák, *Pictorial Architecture*, 1922

János Máttis-Teutsch, *Untitled*, 1925

MEDIUM
Oil and silver paint on canvas

László Moholy-Nagy *Born* 1895 Bácsborsod, Hungary
Died 1946

Lissitzky, El
Proun 12 E, 1923

El Lissitzky made a series of these 'Prouns' – his own little genre of playful, puzzling games of line and plane and geometric form – whose name was supposedly an acronym for 'Projects For the Affirmation of the New' in Russian. They constituted, he said, a meeting-point between art and architecture. That such a meeting was desirable went without saying in the political context of the time: art was idle, but architecture was constructive. In the years following the Revolution, building was the predominant activity in the Soviet Union, in both the most literal and the most metaphorical of senses. Apartment blocks were being built to rehouse the people, the economic infrastructure was being modernized, a new society was actively under construction. As proclaimed by Vladimir Tatlin, Constructivism gave the artist a real part to play in this great venture – his or her contribution could be made on an equal footing with other workers. Lissitzky's Prouns were directly inspired by this excitement, this will to build, but they transcend the immediate context that produced them. Long after the edifice of Soviet Communism came crashing down, they appear as fresh as ever, thanks to their classic poise, ingenuity and wit.

MOVEMENT

Constructivism

SIMILAR WORKS

Varvara Stepanova, *Figure*, 1921

MEDIUM

Oil on canvas

Eliezer (El) Lissitzky *Born* near Smolensk, Russia

Died 1941

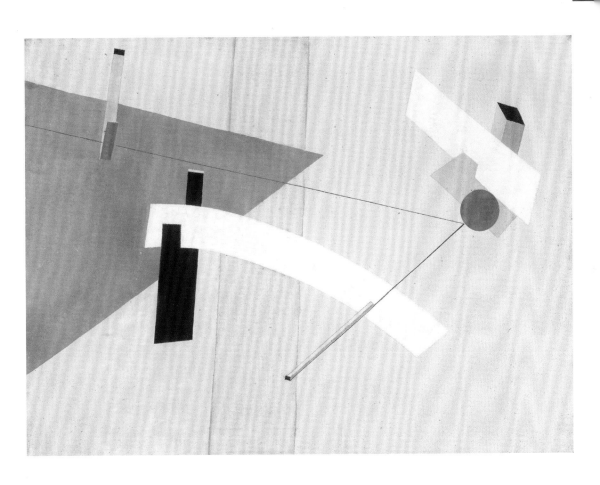

Le Corbusier
(Jeanneret, Charles Edouard)

Still Life With Many Eyes, 1923

Courtesy of Private Collection/www.bridgeman.co.uk/© FLC/ADAGP, Paris and DACS, London 2005

No single individual did more to shape the physical fabric of twentieth-century society than 'Le Corbusier', prophet of a high-tech future and proponent of the 'International Style' in architecture. Applying his enthusiasm for all things industrial to the routine rhythms of everyday existence, he famously insisted that the house should be a 'machine for living'; he attacked the taste for ornament, instead elevating all that was sparse and functional. His theories inspired hundreds of shapely structures in steel, concrete and glass. But before he made the architectural interventions for which he would become famous, Jeanneret was making a modest but influential impact as a painter. In 1918, with his friend, the French painter Amédée Ozenfant (1886–1966), he launched a new movement that he called 'Purism'. Ornamentation was out, and the same fascination with mechanization was evident. 'The picture is a machine for the transmission of sentiments,' they asserted.

MOVEMENT

Purism

SIMILAR WORKS

Amédée Ozenfant, *Still Life: Dishes*, 1920

MEDIUM

Oil on canvas

Charles Edouard Jeanneret *Born* 1887 Switzerland

Died 1965

Man Ray

The Eye in the Keyhole – Composition II, 1928

Man Ray's entrée into Surrealism was in the production of his so-called Rayograms in which he exposed ordinary objects to photosensitive paper using a light source. By this means, objects and the shadows they cast appeared as white ghost-like silhouettes and, because of the high degree of chance and accident in the work, André Breton welcomed Man Ray's work as supportive of Surrealism's ideals.

However, Man Ray's work was not limited to photography and collage and he was involved in the difficulties associated with Surrealism and painting, which manifested themselves in the mid 1920s. These difficulties concerned the interpretation in paint of what was, after all, a literary movement. Following an opening salvo by the artist Max Morise (1903–73), Breton responded in a number of articles in the journal *La Révolution Surréaliste*, in which he laid out some of the criteria for Surrealist painting. Breton maintained that 'The eye exists in a primitive stage' and that 'a painting must open onto something beyond its appearance'. Man Ray's response to this were a number of paintings such as *The Eye in the Keyhole – Composition II*, in which Breton's criteria are met in this voyeuristic enigma that hints of the fetishistic object beyond the keyhole.

MOVEMENT

Dada and Surrealism

SIMILAR WORKS

Salvador Dalí, *The Enigma of Desire*, 1929

MEDIUM

Oil on Canvas

Man Ray *Born* 1890 Philadelphia, USA

Died 1976

Picasso, Pablo

Mandolin and Guitar – Juan les Pins, 1924

Courtesy of Solomon R. Guggenheim Museum, New York, USA/www.bridgeman.co.uk/© Succession Picasso/ DACS 2005

The fusion of styles that became a feature of Picasso's work are evident in *Mandolin and Guitar – Juan les Pins*. The stringed musical instruments played a vital role as a motif in the Analytical Cubism of his work during the period 1910–11. His collages and papier collé from 1912 contain ready-made elements of modern life such as newspapers, bus tickets and fragments of sheet music, as well as detritus such as wood shavings, string and sand. For Picasso, these fragments of modern life were a new form of representation that was not only reinterpretive of pictorial space, but also offered a new visual language in which objects functioned as signs. The subsequent period of Picasso's oeuvre is known as Synthetic Cubism in which he developed more considered ways of pictorial meaning, by, for example, using a more colourful palette to express his ideas. Picasso stated, 'I paint things as I think them not as I see them'.

Mandolin and Guitar – Juan les Pins was painted on the cusp of his involvement with Surrealism in which André Breton claimed Picasso as 'one of ours' in his article *Le Surréalisme et la Peinture* published in its entirety in 1928.

MOVEMENT

Synthetic Cubism

SIMILAR WORKS

René Magritte, *Personal Values*, 1925

MEDIUM

Oil and sand on canvas

Pablo Picasso *Born* 1881 Málaga, Spain

Died 1973

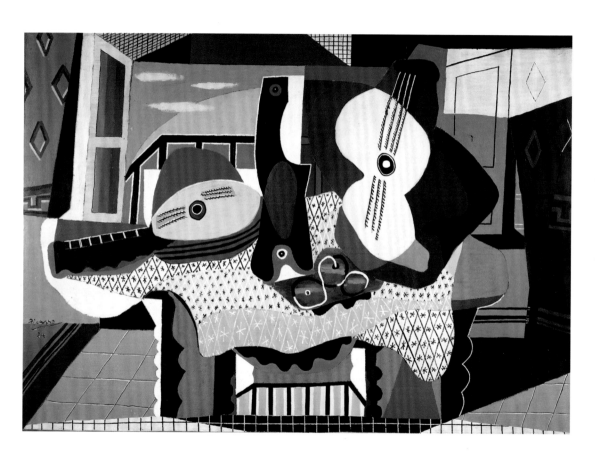

Dupas, Jean

Les Perruches ('The Parrots'), 1925

During the Art Deco period, the rise of the artist-decorator led to the development of a new area of design. Artist-decorators often began their careers in workshops, as skilled artisans in fields such as ironwork, upholstery or cabinet-making. Alternatively, they were industrial artists, the product of specialist schools that had been established to develop art and design in Europe after the British Great Exhibition of 1851.

At the Paris Exhibition in 1925, one of the greatest artist-decorators of the Art Deco period, Jacques-Emile Ruhlmann, unveiled the apogee of interior design: the *Hôtel d'un Collectioneur*. Designed by Pierre Patout (1879–1965), this French pavilion was laid out as a suite of elegant rooms with a vast oval room at its centre: the Grand Salon. Ruhlmann created the interior design and he garnered the help of leading designers of the day to fill it with their artefacts. Jean Dunand (1877–1942), Edgar Brandt (1880–1960) and Antoine Bourdelle (1861–1929) were amongst those leading lights of the day who contributed to this apotheosis of design. Jean Dupas' painting of *Les Perruches* was a focal point of the Grand Salon. Colourful, sumptuous, elegant and refined, the Grand Salon was lauded when it was first unveiled and is now regarded as one of the finest achievements of the French Art Deco period.

MOVEMENT

Art Deco

SIMILAR WORKS

Araignée: table in Macassar and ivory by Jacques-Emile Ruhlmann displayed in the Grand Salon, 1918-19

MEDIUM

Oil on canvas

Jean Dupas *Born* 1882 Lyon, France

Died 1964

van Doesburg, Theo

Contra-Composition of Dissonances, XVI, 1925

'The object of nature is man,' wrote Theo van Doesburg in 1919. 'The object of man is style.' The aphorism sums up De Stijl succinctly, but needs unpacking. Style, van Doesburg suggested, as 'positively expressed in modern plasticity', was a 'well-balanced proportion between peculiarity and generalness'. Too great a concern with the surface, as exemplified in representational art, distracted attention from the inner spirituality of things. Art, he felt, should not be about objectivity but transcendence; beauty lay not in verisimilitude but balance. *De Stijl*, as we have seen, saw the universe as being organized in geometric forms, from which essentials the irregularities of observed reality were only a distraction. The task before the artist was to offer glimpses of that underlying equilibrium in pictures that would inspire viewers to strive to bring about a similar balance in their lives, their society and their built environment. This was an evangelizing art, then, which conducted itself very much as a religion, even to the extent of having schisms – Mondrian left the movement in 1925, apparently affronted at van Doesburg's unorthodox use of diagonals.

MOVEMENT

De Stijl

SIMILAR WORKS

Piet Mondrian, *Composition in Colour A*, 1917

MEDIUM

Oil on canvas

Theo van Doesburg (born Christiaan Küppers) *Born* 1883 Utrecht, Netherlands

Died 1931

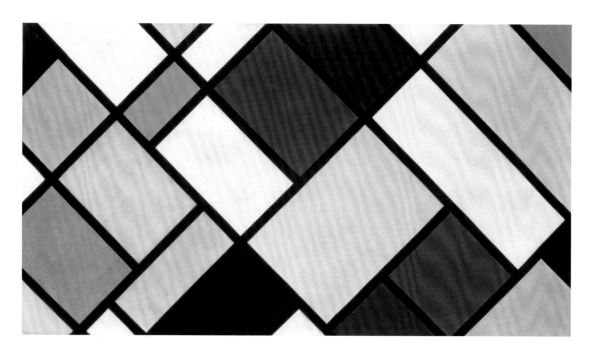

Miró, Joan

Peinture, 1926

When Joan Miró arrived in Paris from Barcelona in 1920, he was fortunate that within a few months he found an empty studio that was next door to André Masson, bringing him into contact with the avant-garde. However, he also spent time in the Louvre looking at the masters including Leonardo da Vinci (1452–1519). From Leonardo's work, Miró would have been made aware of the use of random and chance stains that are often incorporated in his work as a part of the creative process. This, of course, came at a time when Automatism was being discussed in the group around André Breton.

Peinture is a work based on Breton's notions of 'automatic' writing. In 1925, following Breton's *Manifesto of Surrealism*, Miró produced a small drawing entitled *Photo – that is the Colour of my Dreams* in which he placed a single smudged blue dot on a plain ground with the words of the title written in calligraphy. Margit Rowell, a former curator at the Museum of Modern Art in New York, has suggested it is a visual conception of Mallarme's poem '*Un coup de des jamais n'abolira le hazard*', which loosely translated means 'One toss of the dice will never abolish chance'. In *Peinture*, aptly named as devoid of anecdote, the colour blue becomes the actual subject of the work, namely of his dreams.

MOVEMENT

Automatism

SIMILAR WORKS

Hans Arp, *Still Life: Table, Mountain, Anchors and Navel*, 1926

MEDIUM

Oil on canvas

Joan Miró *Born* 1893 Barcelona, Spain

Died 1983

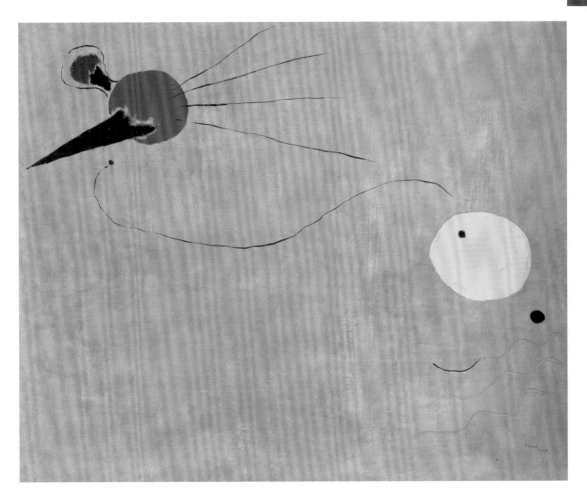

Delaunay, Robert

Triomphe de Paris, 1928–29

Courtesy of Christie's Images/© L&M Services B.V. Amsterdam 2005/0512

'As for our work,' wrote Robert Delaunay to Wassily Kandinsky in 1912, 'I think that surely the public will have to get used to it. The effort it will have to make comes slowly because it is drowned in habits.' In truth, the art-loving public would never really feel at home with Orphism, in theory at least; in practice, paradoxically, it was easy to relate to.

Named after Orpheus, the lyre-playing bard of Greek legend, Orphism was originally a tendency within French Cubism. It was identified around 1912 by a non-painter, the poet Apollinaire: the fact that it was arguably projected on to the art of Delaunay and his circle by an outsider did not make it any easier to understand. The Orphists themselves embraced the label gladly, although quite what it meant was never certain, beyond the fact that it sought to offset the diagrammatic quality of Cubism with a lyric touch and to attain the 'purity' of expression, unencumbered by meaning, to be found in music. Fortunately there was no need to fathom the thinking to appreciate Orphic painting, which was often, as here, a wonderful symphony of shape and colour.

MOVEMENT

Orphism

SIMILAR WORKS

Frantisek Kupka, *Vertical and Horizontal Planes*, c. 1913–14

MEDIUM

Oil on canvas

Robert Delaunay *Born* 1885 Paris, France

Died 1941

Arp, Hans (Jean)
Head, 1929

Having spent his formative artistic years within conventional academic schooling in Weimar and Paris and then within the *Blaue Reiter* ('Blue Rider') group of Expressionists, Hans Arp became a founder member of the Dadaist group in Zurich from 1916. Now free from academic convention, Arp explored 'biomorphism', a concept of organic forms inspired by nature, which had already found a creative outlet in the Parisian and Belgian Art Nouveau styles at the turn of the century. However, Arp's motivation for his biomorphic work was very different to the stylizations of Art Nouveau's practitioners. Like most artists of this period he was deeply affected by the First World War. For him the biomorphic 'reliefs' that he produced from 1915 were a comment on the unity and salvation of nature, to overcome the mechanized and dysfunctional modern world that he was experiencing.

Arp remained committed to these biomorphic forms throughout his artistic career, as an early Dadaist, Surrealist and later as a Constructivist. His amoeba-like creations of fragmented parts of the human body reflected an equally fragmented world.

MOVEMENT

Dada/Biomorphism

SIMILAR WORKS

Henry Moore, *Mask*, 1929

MEDIUM

Relief

Hans Arp *Born* 1887 Strasbourg, France

Died 1966

de Lempicka, Tamara
La Musicienne, 1929

The paintings of Polish-born artist Tamara de Lempicka have become iconic, representing the sophistication, decadence and superficiality of high society in the Art Deco world. De Lempicka was a celebrity artist who painted other celebrities enjoying the rarefied air of an elitist set in Europe between the wars. While she painted the fashionable, rich or titled, other artists were stretching their medium to its limits: Cubism, Dadaism, Fauvism, Surrealism — these are just some of the highly influential art movements of the first four decades of the twentieth century. It is little wonder that de Lempicka's stylized portraits were not always well-received by her fellow artists.

De Lempicka's glory years were from 1925 to 1940, after which she left Paris to live in America. During this time she produced more than 100 portraits. Her figures were often curvaceous, soft and even erotic in their poses, and juxtaposed against an angular background of skyscrapers. The pictures are often alarmingly superficial: bright colours and draped fabric grab the eye but the personality or emotion of the sitter are rarely evident.

MOVEMENT

Art Deco

OTHER WORKS

Girl with Gloves, 1929, *High Summer*, 1928

MEDIUM

Oil on canvas

Tamara de Lempicka *Born* 1900 Warsaw, Poland

Died 1980

Hopper, Edward

Chop Suey, 1929

The terms 'American Scene' and 'Regionalism' are often used interchangeably and, from a technical point of view, this makes perfect sense. Some artists stayed aloof from what became an ideologically freighted Regionalism, however, and the American Scene description is better reserved for them. Edward Hopper's accounts of an everyday America are peculiarly unsettling. He shows a nation cut off from its productive countryside and from those wide-open spaces celebrated by the Regionalists. Here, sunlight barely makes it through the painted-glass window of an urban restaurant. Reflected from a bare white table, it casts a sickly pallor over the lady facing us: Hopper's figures frequently seem like spectres, making their way through the world like the living dead. Isolated, wrapped up in themselves, they come together in anonymous, transitional locations – motel rooms, diners, deserted offices – conversing without ever apparently making contact. Modernism has romanticized the rootless nature of urban society, seeing something heroic in the individual alone, but Hopper had many of the same hankerings as his Regionalist contemporaries. Set against an ideal of community, of social co-operation, a work such as this one is a vision of the damned.

MOVEMENT

American Scene

MEDIUM

Oil on canvas

Edward Hopper *Born* 1882 Nyack, NY, USA

Died 1967

Dalí, Salvador

The Persistence of Memory, 1931

Courtesy of Museum of Modern Art, New York, USA/www.bridgeman.co.uk/© Salvador Dali, Gala-Salvador Dali Foundation, DACS, London 2005

Before joining the Surrealist group formally in 1929, Salvador Dali imbued his work with a sense of the fantastic and the extraordinary, personified in the work of the Old Masters such as Hieronymus Bosch and in his own time by Giorgio de Chirico. In *The Persitence of Memory*, one of his earlier Surrealist works, Dali was influenced by Bosch's *Garden of Earthly Delights*, which he combined with a Catalan background, a feature of much of his early work. This painting was one of the first Dali executed using his 'paranoid-critical' approach in which he depicts his own psychological conflicts and phobias.

The Persistence of Memory contains a self-portrait over which is draped a 'soft watch'. For Dali, these 'soft watches' represent what he called the 'camembert of time', suggesting that the concept of time had lost all meaning in the unconscious world. The ants crawling over the pocket watch suggest decay, an absurd notion given that the watch is metallic. These 'paranoid-critical' images reflect Dali's reading and absorption of Freud's theories of the unconscious and its access to the latent desires and paranoia of the human mind, such as the unconscious fear of death alluded to in this painting.

MOVEMENT

Surrealism

SIMILAR WORKS

Yves Tanguy, *The Cupboard of Proteus,* 1931

MEDIUM

Oil on canvas

Salvador Dalí *Born* 1904 Figueres, Spain

Died 1989

O'Keeffe, Georgia

Red Hills with White Shell, 1938

The summer visits of Georgia O'Keeffe to New Mexico from 1929 were not with her husband Alfred Stieglitz. They were as a guest of the wealthy socialite Mabel Dodge Luhan who also invited, amongst others, the writer D. H. Lawrence and the photographer Ansel Adams. Luhan and her husband owned Ghost Ranch and it was from there that O'Keeffe made her sorties into the desert with Adams and Mabel's husband.

What attracted O'Keeffe to New Mexico as a leitmotif was the combination of the intense light, strong colours and the vastness of the landscape. She realized the limitations of black and white photography, not just because of the inability to convey colour, but also because the intense light created deep and heavy shadows that diminished the clarity of the landscape forms. *Red Hills with White Shell* shows O'Keeffe's awareness of Wassily Kandinsky's (1866–1944) use of the circle and triangle, as 'something more than geometry'. It is based on the hills and canyons around Ghost Ranch, which continued to be an important source of inspiration. In 1940 she succeeded in buying the property for her own use and she eventually purchased a disused Catholic mission further south of Ghost Ranch, where she settled permanently in 1949, after Stieglitz's death.

MOVEMENT

Expressionism

SIMILAR WORKS

Eileen Agar, *Rocks, Ploumanach, Brittany*, 1936

MEDIUM

Oil on canvas

Georgia O'Keeffe *Born* 1887 Wisconsin, USA

Died 1986

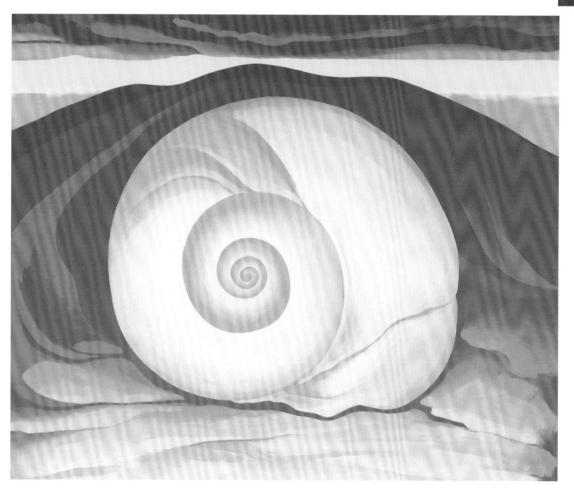

Tanguy, Yves
Composition, 1938

An important aspect of Yves Tanguy's oeuvre was that despite the complexities of some of his works he never used preliminary drawings, relying instead on a high degree of Automatism in the early stages of a painting. His paintings with indeterminate titles, such as *Composition*, have often been likened to seascapes or beach scenes. Tanguy, a native of Brittany, spent time at sea in the merchant navy, as his father had done before him. Writing about Tanguy, André Breton drew on this analogy to describe his paintings: 'The sea ebbs far off disclosing as far as the eye can see sands on which crawl, stand erect, arch, sink and sometimes fly, formations of an entirely new character, without any immediate equivalent in nature, and which, it must be pointed out, have not to this day yielded to any valid interpretation!'

At this time Tanguy began to show rocks in the distance of his pictures, similar to those found on the Brittany coast and which provide the viewer with an immutable foothold on empirical experience. However, the artist sets up a tension in his pictures by including aspects of the ephemeral and illogical, biomorphic shapes that appear familiar, but are subject to change if we lose our concentration.

MOVEMENT

Automatism

SIMILAR WORKS

Roberto Matta, *Rocks*, 1940

MEDIUM

Oil on canvas

Yves Tanguy *Born* 1900 Paris, France

Died 1955

Kahlo, Frida

What the Water Gave Me, 1938

André Breton visited and stayed with Frida Kahlo and her husband Diego Rivera during his visit to Mexico in 1938, acknowledging that she was a self-invented Surrealist. The fact that Breton wrote the preface to Kahlo's exhibition did not qualify her as a Surrealist; in fact, she eschewed the term. Although her pictorial fantasies are often associated with a Surrealist aesthetic, she painted not her dreams or imagination but what she saw as her own nightmarish reality.

In 1925 a serious road-traffic accident left her very badly disabled. Often confined to a hospital bed for weeks undergoing reconstructive surgery, she constructed an image of 'Two Fridas' in order to exorcize the pain and yet maintain a sense of reality. She subsequently discovered that she was unable to conceive children and in a particularly poignant self-portrait, *Henry Ford Hospital* (1932), Kahlo is seen haemorrhaging after suffering a miscarriage. Although her husband Diego Rivera supported her artistically, the relationship was always very tense, overshadowed by the fact that Rivera was Mexico's most famous living artist. Kahlo depicted this dominance in the painting *Frida and Diego Rivera* (1931), while their separation and her subsequent loneliness was depicted in *The Two Fridas* (1939).

MOVEMENT

Surrealism

SIMILAR WORKS

Léonor Fini, *The Secret Festival*, 1964

MEDIUM

Oil on canvas

Frida Kahlo *Born* 1907 Coyoacán, Mexico

Died 1954

Chagall, Marc

A Midsummer Night's Dream, 1939

Tiny fairies fly around as Bottom the weaver embraces their Queen, Titania, in Chagall's vision of Shakespeare's *A Midsummer Night's Dream*. The worlds of magic, fantasy and the unreal were spheres in which the Russian-Jewish artist felt very much at home, steeped in the spirituality of his race and in the folklore of his homeland as he was.

He was encouraged in both by Léon Bakst (1866–1924), under whom he studied in St Petersburg for a while before heading west to enrol in the *École de Paris*. All the main movements, from Cubism to Orphism, had an impact on his work, but Chagall persevered until he had developed a style all his own. Deceptively naïve, it tends towards a religious luminosity (Chagall experimented with stained-glass work), but with none of the ecclesiastical solemnity that may seem to imply. His work is often playful and fanciful, but its charming fairy-tale quality should not blind us to the fact that it often dealt seriously with the great tragedies of existence. Although as good-humoured in art as he was in life, Chagall was a deeply serious artist and one of the most important of his time.

MOVEMENT

École de Paris

SIMILAR WORKS

Léon Bakst, *Set Design for the Ballet Schéhérazade*, 1910

MEDIUM

Oil on canvas

Marc Chagall *Born* 1887 Vitebsk, Russia

Died 1985

Masson, André

Antilles, 1943

Key to understanding André Masson's work is how it and 'automatic' Surrealism differ from their contemporaries, not just within the movement but also, more especially, within Western painting. Masson explained that he began without an image or even a plan in his mind, relying on 'impulses' to direct him, which led him to view the emergence of the marks to give order to the composition. In a meeting he had in the 1930s, he explained this to Henri Matisse (1869–1954) who took a diametrically opposed view in his own work, saying that he took a motif as his starting point, but at the end he had moved so far away from it that he was hardly aware of the subject any more.

In the early 1940s New York had become, for a while, the centre of Surrealism, facilitated by the opening of Peggy Guggenheim's Art of this Century gallery. Masson's 'automatic' work of the 1940s informed a younger generation of artists who were to form the group of artists that became Abstract Expressionists. Like Masson, they were moved to use paint as an expression of their unconscious or inner self that was not a representation of a motif.

MOVEMENT

Surrealism/Automatism

SIMILAR WORKS

Willem de Kooning, *Pink Angel, c.* 1947

MEDIUM

Oil tempera and sand on canvas

André Masson *Born* 1896 Balagny-sur-Thérain, France

Died 1987

Gorky, Arshile

Untitled, 1946

Arshile Gorky was an unashamed plagiarist who nevertheless helped to influence the postwar American art of the Abstract Expressionists. Gorky borrowed very heavily from the Surrealist work of Joan Miró and more particularly Roberto Matta in developing his idiosyncratic style of painting. His work combined Automatism with compositional discipline and saw him tirelessly reuse the same composition, only altering the paint handling or use of colour. To the untrained eye, Gorky's work appeared abstract, with no reference to outside sources. But his use of complex washes of paint often hid the detailed and structurally relevant drawings underneath. As with much American work from this period on, Gorky acted as his own apologist, creating an aura about him and his work based on myth. As an Armenian refugee escaping Turkish tyranny at the end of the First World War, Gorky claimed to have been a disciple and student of Wassily Kandinsky (1866–1944), even to the Museum of Modern Art's acquisitions committee. He also claimed to be a relative of the Russian writer Maxim Gorky, from whom he 'borrowed' his name, not realizing ironically that his name was in fact a pseudonym.

MOVEMENT

Automatism

SIMILAR WORKS

Joan Miró, *Constellation: Awakening at Dawn*, 1941

MEDIUM

Oil on canvas

Arshile Gorky *Born* 1904 Khorkum, Armenia

Died 1948

Calder, Alexander

Untitled, 1947

Courtesy of Christie's Images Ltd/© ARS, NY and DACS, London 2005

It is not hard to see the influence of Joan Miró in this work , in its composition and use of colour and shape. Although American born, Alexander Calder began visiting Paris from 1926 on, where he met Miró and Paul Klee. Having met Piet Mondrian (1872–1944) in a subsequent sojourn, he was invited to join *Abstraction-Création* alongside Naum Gabo and Hans Arp. It was from these meetings and influence that he exhibited his first 'construction'. Although he remained committed to Abstract art, his work is imbued with many of the qualities of a Surrealist aesthetic. Calder replaced his purely Constructivist ideas with more biomorphic forms, his shapes being informed by dream-like forms accessed in the unconscious, rather like Miró's. However, Calder's images are also imbued with humour, an aspect often lacking in Miró's paintings and more often found in Klee's work. The smiling moon in *Untitled* is borrowed from a similar motif used by Klee, for example in *Clown* (1929) and *Senecio* (1922).

Because Calder knew many of the European Surrealists at first hand, his home in Roxbury, Connecticut, was a natural magnet for the émigrés when they arrived in the late 1930s and early 1940s, becoming something of an outpost for the movement.

MOVEMENT

Surrealism/Biomorphism

SIMILAR WORKS

Joan Miró, *Constellation*, 1941

MEDIUM

Oil on canvas

Alexander Calder *Born* 1898 Pennsylvania, USA

Died 1976

Pollock, Jackson

Number 6, 1948

'New arts need new techniques', Jackson Pollock told an interviewer in 1950. 'The modern artist cannot express this age, the airplane, the atom bomb, the radio, in the old forms of the Renaissance or of any other past culture.' How far any of these things were expressed in the splashes and squiggles of 'Jack the Dripper' has of course been hotly debated ever since. His real object was not to depict his age but to express its preoccupations and its energy. The means he found to do this became known as 'Action Painting' because, rather as *Art Informel* had done, it placed its emphasis on the actions and gestures by which the paint was applied and the picture made. Laying out his working surfaces flat on the floor — that way he felt he could approach them from any and every direction without privileging a particular orientation — Pollock dribbled wet paint with a stick or directly from the can. He is guilty as charged of creating nonsense, in that his paintings offer no articulate meaning, but they are fraught with energy, tension, passion and drama. .

MOVEMENT

Abstract Expressionism

SIMILAR WORKS

Willem de Kooning, *Composition*, 1955

MEDIUM

Oil on paper laid down on canvas

Jackson Pollock *Born* 1912 Cody, WY, USA

Died 1956

Lowry, L. S.
The Canal Bridge, 1949

One of modern Britain's best-loved painters, L. S. Lowry was unapproachable in person; he painted happy crowds, but was himself a sad and solitary figure. He was isolated geographically too, spending his whole life in Manchester, well away from metropolitan London where the cultural running was supposedly being made. Despite this he was anything but parochial in his attitude to art. Neither was he the self-taught genius of legend: he studied intermittently yet seriously for over 20 years, many of them under the tutelage of the French painter Adolphe Valette (1876–1942).

Although his works betray the influence of the earlier Camden Town Group, his melancholy humour is all his own. He had a distinctive ambivalence towards his fellow men and women, whom he seems to have loved, but preferred in the undifferentiated anonymity of the crowd. He painted an urban industrial landscape that we are accustomed to regard as grim, but which in his work appears positively picturesque.

MOVEMENT

Camden Town Group

SIMILAR WORKS

Robert Bevan, *Horse Dealers (Sale at Ward's Repository, No. 1)*, 1918

Charles Isaac Ginner, *Bethnal Green Allotment*, c. 1943

MEDIUM

Oil on canvas

Laurence Stephen Lowry *Born* 1887 Manchester, England

Died 1976

Bacon, Francis
Head VI, 1949

Velasquez, Bacon suggested, really believed he was recording the court of his time; however, photography and philosophy had put paid to that idea between them. Offering accurate representations instantaneously, the former had usurped the artist's role as chronicler of unfolding lives, while the latter had called into question the very nature of existence. The artist, Bacon concluded, could no longer delude himself that he was fixing any sort of reality; art, he said, had become 'a game by which man distracts himself'. It was thus its own inspiration and provided its own motive and force: every painting was an 'accident', he believed. The very application of the paint transformed the conception of the work as it went along, with the finished painting representing its own reality. Hence, the head shown here has its own artistic integrity, although clearly incomplete from a conventionally realistic point of view. Along with Lucian Freud (b. 1922), Leon Kossoff (b. 1926), Frank Auerbach (b. 1931) and others, Bacon belonged to what became known as the School of London. This was a more-than-usually arbitrary designation, for while Bacon was a social animal – even a hell-raiser – artistically he walked alone.

MOVEMENT

Existential Art/School of London

SIMILAR WORKS

Graham Sutherland, *Thorn Head*, 1946

MEDIUM

Oil on canvas

Francis Bacon *Born* 1909 Dublin, Ireland

Died 1992

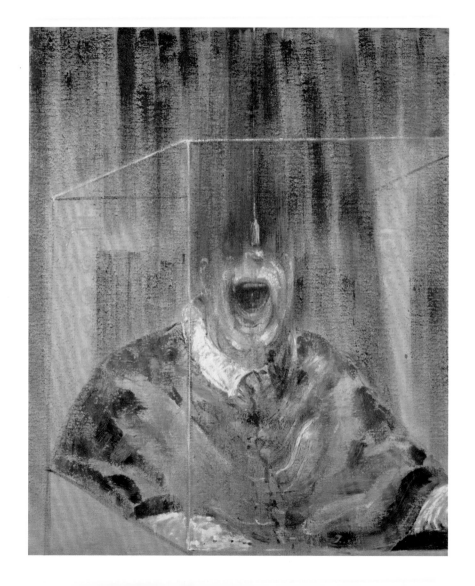

Rothko, Mark

Untitled, 1951

To confront a Mark Rothko work such as this one is to feel caught up in a real confrontation. Critic David Sylvester has remarked on the 'emphatic frontality' of the artist's work. 'We are', he writes, 'faced with a highly ambiguous presence which seems, on the one hand, ethereal, empty, on the other solid and imposing, like a megalith.' It possesses, Sylvester concludes, the sort of sublimity to be found in a wild landscape and clearly springs from the Romantic tradition in western art.

More technically, works in this style are known as 'Colour Field Painting' because the work is seen as a single, continuous field without obvious focus or compositional hierarchy. The term derives from 'Field Painting', which attempted to achieve a comparable effect with abstract forms. Helen Frankenthaler's 'stain painting' (see page 138) was to take this style another step further in the 1960s. Yet Sylvester is surely right: Rothko is a Romantic and the essence of his work escapes such analysis. No real work of art can satisfactorily be summed up in technical terms, perhaps, but the attempt in Rothko's case falls especially short.

MOVEMENT

Abstract Expressionism/Colour Field Painting

SIMILAR WORKS

Hans Hofmann, *The Gate*, 1959–60

Adolph Gottlieb, *Three Discs*, 1960

MEDIUM

Acrylic on canvas

Mark Rothko (born Marcus Rothkowitz) *Born* 1903 Dvinsk, Russia

Died 1970

Freud, Lucian

Head of a Boy, 1954

From the point of view of technique, this could be seen as a Realist – even Superrealist – portrait, but there is an 'in-your-face' quality about this particular face that disconcerts. Utterly conventional in apparent essentials, it is nevertheless profoundly and unaccountably unsettling, and that is the Freud effect in a nutshell. It had been so ever since he made his artistic breakthrough in 1951 with *Interior at Paddington* (now in the Walker Art Gallery, Liverpool) and has continued to be so to this day. A certain washed-out pallor contributes to the effect in this painting, as does the subtly lopsided impression given by the nose and upper lip. More important, perhaps, is the slightly shifty way in which the subject avoids our gaze: this is a work that, albeit very quietly, breaks the rules.

Like his friend Francis Bacon, Lucian Freud is associated with the School of London, although once again the label tells us little about his work. His German-Jewish father, Ernst, an architect and son of the founder of psychoanalysis, Sigmund Freud, brought Lucian to England in 1932 when he was still a boy.

MOVEMENT

Existential Art/School of London

SIMILAR WORKS

Michael Andrews, *Study of a Man in a Landscape (Digswell)*, 1959

Leon Kossoff, *Leon Kossoff*, 1981

MEDIUM

Oil on canvas

Lucian Freud *Born* 1922 Berlin, Germany

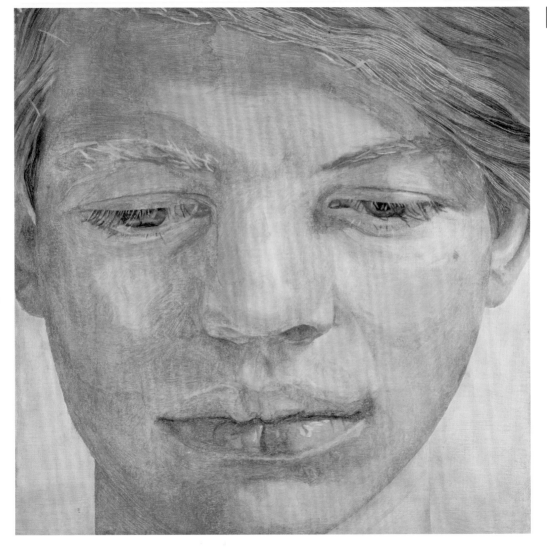

de Kooning, Willem

Marilyn Monroe, 1954

Willem de Kooning's Abstract Expressionism was not necessarily completely abstract, although the film star has been swept up into an emotion greater and wilder than her own iconic image here. The precise nature of that emotion, and whether it is as a positive or negative one, is altogether harder to pin down.

An earlier series by de Kooning (*Woman I–VI*, 1950–52) had already incurred the wrath of doctrinaire critics who felt that the figurative age in art had gone. It was subsequently to attract criticism from feminist critics, too. Taken to extremes (as occasionally it has been), the case against them was that these works represented their subjects as dehumanized puppets and, worse, that they were painted in such a violent flurry of ungoverned brushstrokes as to amount to the artistic equivalent of a frenzied knife attack. Such judgements are subjective, of course: if de Kooning's picture is indeed informed by a deep-seated misogyny, it still offers a revealing and disturbing insight into 1950s culture. In addition, however negative its passion, it offers a profound ironic contrast to the empty shell of celebrity that is paraded in Andy Warhol's (1928–87) Marilyn prints.

MOVEMENT

Abstract Expressionism

SIMILAR WORKS

Arshile Gorky, *Betrothal II*, 1947

MEDIUM

Oil on canvas

Willem de Kooning *Born* 1904 Rotterdam, Netherlands

Died 1967

Albers, Josef

Homage, 1954

Josef Albers taught at the Bauhaus before the Nazis closed it down in 1933, whereupon he and his wife Anni went to the United States as refugees. Both became teachers at North Carolina's famous Black Mountain College where they brought the skills and insights of the Bauhaus to a generation of young American artists. In 1950 Josef became head of the design department at Yale University – he was a distinguished academic, producing notable works on colour theory.

All this time he remained a working artist too, devoting himself to a long series of paintings collectively titled 'Homage to the Square'. This shape was particularly worthy of reverence, he felt, because exemplifying the ultimate in flatness and regularity it was the most quintessentially artificial, and thus artistic, of forms, the farthest possible from nature. Typically, as here, he set squares within one another, their subtly differentiated shades and tones creating distortions in apparent size. This aspect of his work offers parallels with some of the work being done by the Op Artists, one of whom, Richard Anuszkiewicz (b. 1930), was a student of his.

MOVEMENT

Bauhaus/Op Art

SIMILAR WORKS

Richard Anuszkiewicz, *Trolley-Stop Still Life*, 1952

MEDIUM

Oil on canvas

Josef Albers *Born* 1888 Westphalia, Germany

Died 1976

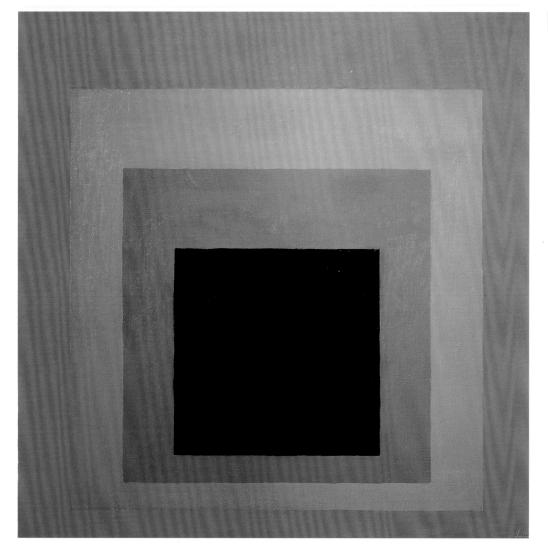

Prévert, Jacques
The Aeroplane, 1957

In 1924 the Nobel laureate writer Anatole France died. Considered by many to be one of the greatest Classically based writers ever, he was not equally revered by André Breton, who considered his work vulgar in its use of language. Although France shared many political ideals with the Surrealists, they considered that his empathy was one of pure self-interest. Breton, with contributions from some of the other Surrealist writers, wrote his own satirical eulogy entitled '*Un Cadavre*' ('The Corpse'), stating 'Let us not forgive him' in a parody of the endless eulogies being heaped on the late writer.

By the late 1920s there was dissention within the ranks of the Surrealists, with a new group around Georges Bataille, which included Robert Desnos and Jacques Prévert, offering an alternative literary set that was less dogmatic in its approach. By this time Breton had become something of a control freak within the original group and the dissenters published their own response to Breton's earlier '*Un Cadavre*'. Using the same title, the group published a critique of Breton in early 1930 in which they accused him of turning Surrealism into a religion, of which he was the self-styled 'Pope'.

MOVEMENT

Surrealism

SIMILAR WORKS

René Magritte, *Time Transfixed*, 1939

MEDIUM

Collage

Jacques Prévert *Born* 1900 Paris, France

Died 1977

Kline, Franz

Provincetown II, 1959

'The final test of a painting ...', said Franz Kline, is 'Does the painter's emotion come across?' His works are intensely felt, even by the standards of Abstract Expressionism. This movement of the 1950s and 1960s rejected both Realism and the more geometric forms of abstract art: the painter's task was to represent not objects, scenes or patterns, but emotions. Kline saw his paintings as 'situations': his first brushstroke set in motion a drama that he then wrestled to resolve. The sense of struggle in his work is thrilling, and his most famous works seem like epic battles of black and white; only in his last years did he move to incorporate a much greater range of colours.

It had not always been thus: as a young man, Kline had gone to England to pursue a decorous interest in nineteenth-century illustration. His own works of the 1930s were of a piece with this – conservative, even genteel – but all that changed when he met Willem de Kooning (1904–97) in 1943. He was transfixed by the Dutchman's genius, and his own art was transformed: Kline became one of the boldest artists of his generation.

MOVEMENT

Abstract Expressionism

SIMILAR WORKS

Willem de Kooning, *Composition*, 1955

MEDIUM

Oil on canvas

Franz Kline *Born* 1910 Wilkes-Barre, PA, USA

Died 1962

Escher, M. C.

Ascending and Descending, 1960

Although M. C. Escher did not belong to any Surrealist group, his work shares its aesthetic language if not an idealist or motivational one. His work before about 1937 is based on observations of reality, depicted as a kind of super-reality in the exaggerated use of line to emphasize a key aspect of the motif. For example in *St Peter's Rome* (1935) the view is from inside the dome of the church. By exaggerating the angle of the view towards the ground, one that could not possibly have been taken from reality, the viewer is presented with a vertiginous headlong plummet to the marble floor.

His work post 1937 is from a period when he was forced to flee to Switzerland, avoiding the imminent build-up of Fascist troops in Italy, where he had been living until then and which had been such an inspiration for his 'architectural' drawings. After this time Escher had to rely more on memory and imagination and so began to create more playful forms of spatial exploration. These were based on his observations of the regular divisions of the plane at the Alhambra, which prompted an investigation of the mathematical principles behind it.

MOVEMENT

Superrealism

SIMILAR WORKS

François Morellet, *Sphère-Trame*, 1962

MEDIUM

Lithograph

Maurits Cornelis Escher *Born* 1898 Leeuwarden, Netherlands

Died 1972

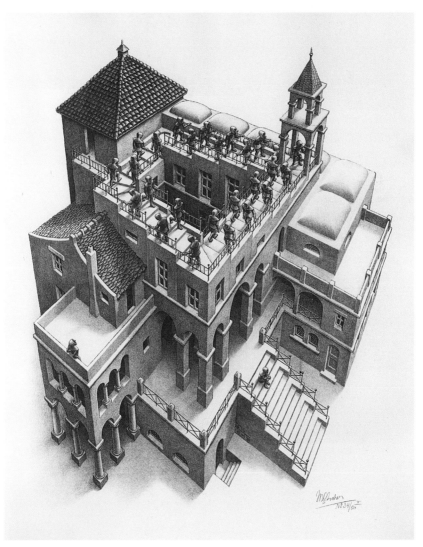

Agar, Eileen

Lewis Carroll with Alice, 1960–62

Although this is an oil painting, *Lewis Carroll with Alice* is clearly based on collage, using a wide range of shapes and colours to build up the mosaic-like image, possibly inspired by Nusch Eluard's use of the medium in the mid 1930s to express the correlation of women to nature. This work includes reference to the English landscape and its connotations of nature, a key motif in the work of Eileen Agar, following a brief but inspirational love affair with Paul Nash, while she lived close to him and his wife in Dorset.

The motif of 'Alice' can of course be seen within the context of the *femme-enfant*, but in English Surrealism, Lewis Carroll's 'Alice' already retained a special place within the British Romantic tradition. The critic Herbert Read, who fell at the first hurdle in trying to explain Surrealism, or as he called it 'Super-realism', to the British public, continually saw the aesthetic within the Romantic tradition. Read, a modernist who critically supported, amongst others, Nash and Henry Moore, had more of an affinity with Abstraction, which probably explains Agar's use of geometric shapes in what is essentially a Surrealist work.

MOVEMENT

Surrealism

SIMILAR WORKS

Rita Kernn-Larsen, *Self Portrait*, 1937

MEDIUM

Oil on canvas

Eileen Agar *Born* 1899 Buenos Aires, Argentina

Died 1991

Lichtenstein, Roy

Eddie Diptych, 1962

Courtesy of The Art Archive/Dagli Orti/© The Estate of Roy Lichtenstein/DACS 2005

Since Pop Art took the imagery of mass culture as its subject, it was drawn irresistibly to the mass media by which that culture was transmitted. Many artists created stupendous works in montage, using ready-made images, but Roy Lichtenstein famously went further. Magnifying the frames of cheap strip cartoons to many times their original size, he fashioned them into works of art in the classic mould, painting in their Ben Day dots with loving detail through a special paper stencil.

In doing so he took the most stereotypical of images and the most hackneyed of sentiments and placed them on the pedestal previously reserved for the 'highest' art. Here, for example, in the drama of the jilted girl, he has created a 'diptych', a hinged two-panel painting of a sort associated with medieval religious art. This 'cod-canonification' undoubtedly brought out the banality of the strips that had inspired them, but Lichtenstein's purpose was certainly not to sneer. Indeed, he admired his models and aspired to replicate in conventional art the impersonal perfection he found in such mass-produced, industrially printed media, and in this respect he anticipated the Superrealists.

MOVEMENT

Pop Art

SIMILAR WORKS

James Rosenquist, *World's Fair Mural*, 1963–64

MEDIUM

Oil and acrylic

Roy Lichtenstein *Born* 1923 New York, USA

Died 1997

I TRIED TO REASON IT OUT! I TRIED TO SEE THINGS FROM MOM AND DAD'S VIEW-POINT! I TRIED NOT TO THINK OF EDDIE, SO MY MIND WOULD BE CLEAR AND COMMON SENSE COULD TAKE OVER! BUT EDDIE KEPT COMING BACK...

Frankenthaler, Helen

The Bay, 1963

'Stain painting' is one of several movements arguably spawned by Abstract Impressionism, but impatient with its overt emotionalism. Painters such as De Kooning, Kline and Mark Rothko had brought an almost religious intensity to their work, an earnestness with which a younger generation found itself uneasy. The 1950s had seen the coming of 'Cool Jazz' on to the music scene: elegant, mellow and effortlessly accomplished. Younger painters set out to embody those qualities in art.

Helen Frankenthaler found a way of letting the paint do all the work, pouring it directly on to the canvas, and then letting it spread out where it would. Where Jackson Pollock had poured thick paint, however, she thinned hers so that it would spread out more freely and be absorbed into the canvas, a technique to which she gave the name of 'soak-stain'. The difference is significant, with implications not only for the size of the resulting stain, but for the relationship between the paint and its background. The two interpenetrated in Frankenthaler's works, colour and canvas inseparably integrated to produce a somehow complete and satisfying work of art.

MOVEMENT

Post-painterly Abstraction/Green Mountain Boys

SIMILAR WORKS

Morris Louis, *Beth Chaf*, 1959

Kenneth Noland, *Half*, 1959

MEDIUM

Acrylic on canvas

Helen Frankenthaler *Born* 1928 New York, USA

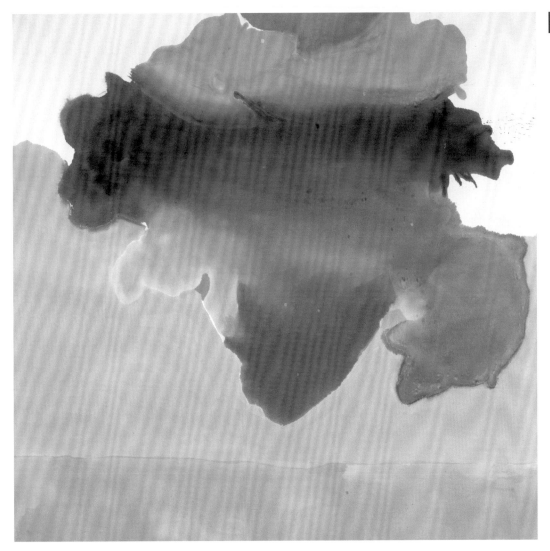

Hockney, David

Cleanliness is Next to Godliness, 1965

With its unalloyed pleasure in all things cheap and tacky, Pop Art is close kin to camp, the aesthetic of what by the 1960s was an increasingly confident gay subculture. In the course of that decade, homosexuality would be decriminalized in Britain and America, and 1969 would see New York's gay community come together for its own defence against official harassment in the 'Stonewall Riots'.

When the young David Hockney left a dreary, rainswept London for Los Angeles in 1963, he went in search not only of sunshine, but also of sex — and self-respect. Attitudes among urban sophisticates in California were far in advance of prevailing values elsewhere. Here it was possible to be a 'gay artist' true to self and sexuality, and with Pop Art fashionable there was a style ready-made. This witty little squib from 1964 shows an attractive hunk half-hidden in a shower, the curtain displaying his body even as it supposedly conceals. The title pokes mischievous fun at the sort of puritanism encapsulated in the old saying: the picture's purpose, of course, is anything but 'clean'.

MOVEMENT

Pop Art

SIMILAR WORKS

Richard Hamilton, *Adonis in Y-Fronts*, 1962–63

Robert Indiana, *Sex Anyone?*, 1964

MEDIUM & DIMENSIONS

Silkscreen in five colours, 36$\frac{1}{2}$ x 23 inches, Ed: 40

David Hockney *Born* 1937 Bradford, England

Delvaux, Paul

Les Adieux, 1964

A major theme of Surrealist activity was desire, often depicting women as its object. Its male practitioners believed that women were closer to the irrationality of dreams and the latent portent of their significance within the unconscious. They also believed that women held the key to understanding male desire within that unconscious. In his novel *Nadja*, André Breton related his account of a fleeting but intense relationship he had with the heroine. In the book Breton wore his heart on his sleeve, trying to understand the complexities of his often contradictory feelings for her. *Les Adieux* seems to be a response to that same quest. The males are anonymous, also a recurrent motif of Magritte's, so that our attention is given to the woman bidding her farewells. Her pose is mannered, an impassive and innocent look that conveys no sensuality. We are unable to contemplate her status, her look completely devoid of anecdote or emotion, resembling that of a mannequin.

The candle is something of an enigma, possibly signifying the fleetingness of life. Are her farewells permanent? Is she saying farewell to the men whose destiny is known only to her? The answer to the riddle is available only to people who understand the language of the unconscious.

MOVEMENT

Surrealism

SIMILAR WORKS

René Magritte, *The Ready-made Bouquet*, 1957

MEDIUM

Oil on cardboard

Paul Delvaux *Born* 1897 Anheit, Belgium

Died 1994

Magritte, René

Le Fils de l'homme, 1964

The bowler-hatted man came to personify René Magritte and his relative anonymity, the figure either depicted with his back to the viewer or his face obscured. In *Le Fils de l'homme* we are confronted by such a figure, his face obscured by an apple. This suggests not only the aspect of anonymity but also Magritte grappling with another modernist motif, the theory of relativity. Sir Isaac Newton's theories about gravity or 'the mechanical world view' were called into question following Einstein's theories about space and time, which were published in 1916 and in which he proposed an 'electromagnetic world view'.

. Since Newton's gravitational theories were based on seeing an apple fall to the ground, Magritte positions his apple in suspension and we, the viewer, are unsure whether this is permanent or it is still falling. However, *Le Fils de l'homme* is not just a reflection of scientific progress. Magritte is deliberately subverting any dogmatic view of the physical world by disturbing its empiricist normalcy and questioning the compromise that humans make in reconciling the 'real' world. This plurality of experience, which corresponded with Einstein's Theory of Relativity, abolished the absoluteness of space and time in Newtonian terms, and thus the predictability of life.

MOVEMENT

Surrealism

SIMILAR WORKS

Oscar Dominguez, *Max en bouteille*, 1939

MEDIUM

Oil on canvas

René Magritte *Born* 1898 Lessines, Belgium

Died 1967

Caulfield, Patrick

Sweet Bowl, 1967

The term 'Pop Art' was first used in 1958, anticipating the 1960s revolution in pop music by some years. The phrase was coined by critic Lawrence Alloway: it neatly encapsulated the inspiration, sometimes, but by no means invariably, 'camp' and ironic, that was to be found in commercial art of every kind, from children's cartoons to advertising posters. As developed by friends of Alloway, such as Eduardo Paolozzi (1924–2005), Pop Art was not so very different from the American Neo-Dadaism of Jasper Johns (b. 1930) and Larry Rivers (b. 1923). What changed, in fact, was not so much the art itself as the cultural context. British pop music was taking the world by storm. By the mid-1960s, interest in the Beatles and other pop groups was clearly transcending their primary 'teen' market, and self-conscious sophisticates were taking an interest in their music. In response, performers moved on from the bouncy dance records and sentimental ballads that had made them famous to create self-consciously intellectual records. In music and art alike, pastiche was key: the means by which the clichés of mass culture were raised above the commonplace to the status of 'high' art.

MOVEMENT

Pop Art

SIMILAR WORKS

David Hockney, *Peter Getting Out of Nick's Pool*, 1966–67

MEDIUM

Screen print

Patrick Caulfield *Born* 1936 London, UK

Died 2002

Warhol, Andy

Campbell's Soup, 1968

This world-famous soup tin elbowed Marilyn Monroe into second place as the most immediately recognizable image of the Pop Art era. Warhol arguably did more than any other individual to create the widely held impression that modern art was a lot of nonsense, and few have done as much to keep art at the centre of the cultural stage. He dealt unashamedly in the ephemeral, said notoriously that everyone should be famous for 15 minutes, yet 40 years on, his fame seems set to be enduring. He was never simply a painter: his role was more that of entrepreneur or impresario. Founder of a pop group, the Velvet Underground, and presiding figure in a varied circle of creative painters and sculptors centred on his studio, 'The Factory', he became an unavoidable presence in American and international art of the 1960s.

Was Warhol a great artist, or an artist at all? He has little obviously in common with Leonardo da Vinci or even Pablo Picasso. However, banal as the images with which he works may be, he transmutes them into something altogether stranger and more startling, an artistic achievement by any definition.

MOVEMENT

Pop Art

SIMILAR WORKS

James Rosenquist, *Firepole*, 1966–67

MEDIUM

Screen print

Andy Warhol (born Andrew Warhola) *Born* 1928 Pittsburgh, USA

Died 1987

Stella, Frank

Agbatana II, 1968

There is a clear echo of Kenneth Noland's 'target' paintings in this work. Stella shared many of the older artist's preoccupations, yet over time the ways in which he would explore them would vary greatly. Even so an interest in geometrical forms remained more or less a constant, running through his works from the austere black-and-white 'pinstripe' paintings of the early 1960s to this work of almost carnival colour and humour.

Stella said his use of regular patterns helped him solve 'the painterly problems of what to put here and there and how to do it to make it go with what was there'. The remark was characteristically self-deprecatory, as he is up to dealing with most 'painterly problems' he is likely to encounter, but it chimes in with his wider approach to painting. In the spirit of the Hard-Edge school, Stella is in artistic principle uninterested in solving such problems: he wants his works to stand impersonal, self-contained. 'A good pictorial idea is worth more than a lot of manual dexterity', he maintains – the point of a painting is that it should be an idea embodied.

MOVEMENT

Post-painterly Abstraction/Hard-Edge Painting

SIMILAR WORKS

Al Held, *Hidden Fortress*, 1961

Kenneth Noland, *Drought*, 1962

MEDIUM

Oil on canvas

Frank Stella *Born* 1936 Malden, Mass, USA

Dine, Jim

Flo-Marker Hearts, 1969

The subject matter is very recognizably that of Pop Art, but the effect is altogether more painterly than is to be found in the famous works of Andy Warhol (1928–87) or Roy Lichtenstein (1923–98). It recalls, indeed, the intense canvases of the Abstract Expressionists. A major figure on the Pop Art scene of the 1960s, Dine was a pioneer of the 'Happening', a staged event involving bystanders in a sort of organized spontaneity and the inspiration for later Performance Art.

The nature of such creations is that they are one-offs, their unpredictability and impermanence representing a conscious rejection of old-fashioned artistic conventions by which the artist aspired to complete control and a 'classic' beauty that would transcend time. Jim Dine turns a Janus face to art, embracing the new aesthetic in all its unruliness and its delight in the ephemeral, without relinquishing his concern to create beauty of a more traditional sort. In this he resembles R. B. Kitaj (1927–94), an acknowledged influence, with whom Dine came into contact when both were working in England in the 1960s.

MOVEMENT

Pop Art

SIMILAR WORKS

Ed Ruscha, *Ace*, 1962–63

MEDIUM

Watercolour on paper

Jim Dine *Born* 1935 Cincinnati, OH, USA

Close, Chuck
Linda, 1975–76

Argentinean writer Jorge Luis Borges was all the rage in the 1960s and 1970s, and among his most famous works was the story *Pierre Menard, Author of the Quixote*. A modern writer, Menard set out to recreate Cervantes' masterpiece meticulously. Although every word was identical, the changing context made his a completely different work. Something of the same logic underlies the apparent perversity of the Superrealist project: what appears to be Realism is better seen as an elaborate game of allusion and irony.

Blown up to billboard-size, Chuck Close's portraits have all the impersonality of industrially produced advertising art, along with the intimacy of immediate connection. Many of his sitters are friends and fellow artists and their least blemishes are laboriously captured in loving detail. Like Roy Lichtenstein (1923–97), Close goes to enormous lengths to avoid any suggestion of painterly texture: he transfers a snapshot to a gigantic grid, then works with an airbrush to reproduce the sheer-smooth effects of the photographic original, and its flaws. Here, for example, the photograph's failure to cope with the stream of sunlight on the subject's hair, and the slight loss of focus about the shoulders, are both recreated by Close.

MOVEMENT

Superrealism

SIMILAR WORKS

Audrey Flack, *Lady Madonna*, c. 1972

MEDIUM

Acrylic on canvas

Chuck Close *Born* 1940 Monroe, WA, USA

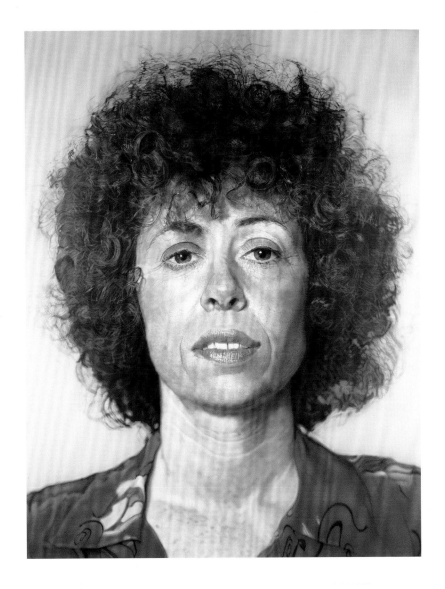

Haring, Keith
Untitled, 1981

Even the most 'legitimate' artists have historically tended to live chaotic, 'Bohemian' lives, and since the Romantic era the raffish demimonde in which they have moved has to some extent been idealized in art and literature. The middle classes have, moreover, always had a way of envying the poor, if not their material privations, then at least their apparent freedom from respectable constraints. Hence the admiration felt by many artists for the untrammelled energy and undoubted ingenuity of the graffiti art that began to emblazon New York's subway trains in the 1970s. Intoxicated by the sense of freedom they found in such art, a number of American artists began to emulate it, both in public places and on canvases of their own. The most famous of these were Keith Haring (1958–90), an out-of-towner from Pennsylvania, and Jean-Michel Basquiat, an African-American artist of middle-class origins. British critics have dismissed Graffiti Art: at best it is bogus, they say; at worst a form of aesthetically sanctioned vandalism. Such criticism misses the main point: whether these intricate scribblings are authentic or not, works of great freshness and originality have been created.

MOVEMENT

Graffiti Art

SIMILAR WORKS

Jean-Michel Basquiat, *Self-Portrait*, 1986

MEDIUM

Oil and acrylic on canvas

Keith Haring *Born* 1958 Kutztown, PA, USA

Died 1990

Hirst, Damien

Painting for Marco Pierre-White, 1996

Marcus Harvey's (b. 1963) *Myra* was *the* sensation of the Royal Academy's 'Sensation' exhibition of 1997. Gazing balefully out from beneath a great bob of peroxide hair in the infamous photograph, 'Moors Murderer' Myra Hindley was one of the great anti-icons of post-war Britain. Just to add insult to injury as far as many were concerned, Harvey's eleven-foot blow-up was composed entirely of children's hand prints.

Was this a calculated outrage? Ever since Damien Hirst launched the exhibition 'Freeze' in a warehouse in London's Docklands in 1988, there had been accusations that 'Britart' began and ended in cheap sensation. London's young artists made no attempt to reject the charge, making play with it instead. While works such as *Myra* and Tracey Emin's *Bed* became the lightning conductors for media-orchestrated outrage, others were getting on with only slightly less controversial work. Hirst himself, the founder of Britart, aroused press opprobrium for a series of animal carcasses bisected and preserved in formaldehyde, and this little still life is, in its way, just as challenging. Simultaneously charming and morbid, a memento mori and a record of cruelty, it sums up the aesthetic and moral ambiguity of great art.

MOVEMENT

Britart/Young British Artists

SIMILAR WORKS

Tracey Emin, *Exploration of the Soul*, 1994

MEDIUM & DIMENSIONS

Gloss household paint and butterflies on canvas, 2 x 2 feet

Damien Hirst *Born* 1965 Bristol, England

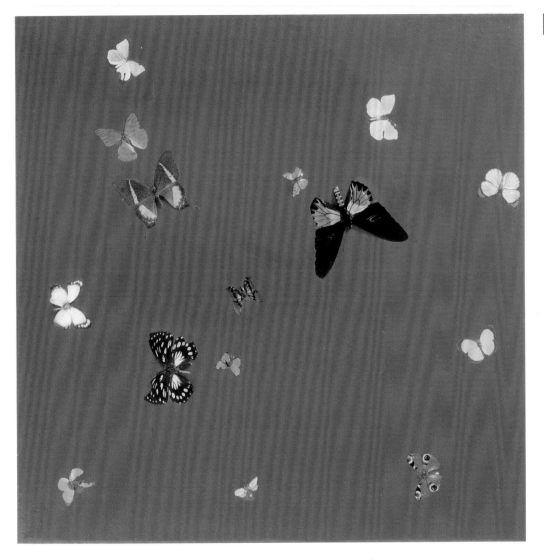

Frost, Terry
Orchard Tambourines, 1999

Courtesy of The Royal Academy of Arts/© Terry Frost Estate/Courtesy of Paragon Press

Terry Frost is regarded as one of postwar Britain's most important abstract painters, though he himself didn't see it quite that way. He set out in his works to depict what he regarded as real scenes. Rather than reproduce the sights before him, however, he sought to capture the 'total experience' of the beholder, emotions and all. 'What I have painted', he said of one work, 'is an arrangement of form and colour that evokes for me a particular feeling.'

Hence the comparison with Abstract Expressionism, which was emerging in the United States at the same time as Frost's artistic career was taking shape at St Ives in the late 1940s and early 1950s. Critic Peter Fuller has suggested that the stars of the American movement drew unacknowledged inspiration from the St Ives School: that claim is controversial, to say the least. It does, however, highlight similarities of preoccupation and technique that can make comparisons between the two as interesting as they are potentially provocative. With its bright and boldly contrasting colours, its regular forms and its unapologetic flatness, this late woodcut has a cheery, even festive air.

MOVEMENT

Abstract Expressionism/St Ives School

SIMILAR WORKS

Peter Lanyon, *Coast*, 1953

MEDIUM

Woodcut print

Terry Frost *Born* 1915 Leamington Spa, England

Died 2003

Index